DATA
FOR
EXECUTIVES

How to influence stakeholders and achieve success

Nick Hobbie

ACCOLADES

G ood data ensures credibility and helps explain the story you're trying to tell.

-**Joe Pressler,** *MBA,BSN,RN*| COO | Healthcare

N ick Hobbie's "Data For Executives" simplifies connecting and communicating the story of your data to an executive audience. As a Lean Six Sigma Black Belt in Food Manufacturing, analyzing data for improvement projects is a critical function of my role. Equally important, though, is conveying that data in a way that is clear and engages the stakeholders and decision makers in my company. "Data For Executives" provides the theory and practical 'how-to' to make that communication effective.

-**Thomas Bucher,** *CSSBB* | Continuous Improvement Manager | Food Manufacturing

D ata For Executives (DFE) is the way to get the edge on captivating your executive audience with ease. DFE pulls together all the key visual components in one place...like visual perception, illuminate color and the most effective visual style medium. Do you want to WOW your leadership and send the correct message to take action? "Don't Stop!" DFE will give you the edge up from the standard data spectrum. Just try it!

-**Penny Campbell** | Senior Provider Contract Coordinator | Healthcare

T he ideas and concepts intricately laid out in this book provide clear guidance to not only present data effectively, but also master the art of persuasion with data. This book provides a step by step template for presenting data in a way that is easy for the audience to digest and understand. It is a must read for anyone who wishes to convey their message with authority and effectiveness.

-**Matt Cohee** | IT Security | Insurance

T his book is literally eye opening. It could prove helpful in any profession involving communication of data in a clear and efficient manner. Nick utilizes both modern and artistic expression in designing a successful presentation. I could see this book being used to train students at a collegiate level.
-**Nathaniel Hiss,** *DC* | Doctor of Chiropractic Medicine| Healthcare

T he book, Data For Executives, is an excellent resource for beginning and experienced presentation developers alike. It is very informative and thought provoking. It is a great combination of data, design and communication for all presenters to understand or start understanding prior to developing their next presentation. This book breaks down how to tell your data story and how to keep the audience focused on the main theme or idea of your story using effective graphs and color schemes. The graph examples are outstanding, what to use, why you use it and what not to use. The use of colors, labels and fonts in designing your presentation is a unique twist compared to other resources. Overall, Data For Executives, is an excellent topic and a valuable resource for anyone in the data communication environment that is working to thrive and succeed in the ever-changing data analytics field.
- **Tim McCrady,** *Lean Six Sigma Master Black Belt* | Process Improvement| Tier 1 Automotive Supplier & Healthcare

D ata is the driving force for change. As healthcare is an ever changing environment, it is crucial to understand how data is best communicated and absorbed for predicting future industry trends. "Data for Executives" provides lucrative insight on how to connect with your audience to best support the numerical, visual, and hard-earned data you've prepared.
-**Allison Schiffli,** *MBA* | Site Supervisor| Healthcare

ISBN 978-1-735-84310-0 (Paperback)
ISBN 978-1-735-84310-1 (ePub)
ISBN 978-1-735-84310-2 (ePDF)

Find more information at our website.
NickHobbie.com

To my wife and kids:
Thank you for coming along on this journey with me. Without your support, I could not have achieved as much as I did.

To my father:
Thank you for your guidance and help during this process.

GET INSPIRED

Within these pages there are multiple examples of colors, graphs, icons, and images with in these pages to help with your inspiration. QR codes, similar to the one below, will direct you to more information on my website. Use your phones QR reader to be redirected. Visit the site for more visuals, colors, and ideas to keep you inspired!.

CHAPTER 1

Data For Executives

You are standing in the front of the boardroom, the projector screen behind you, and the remote in your left hand. This has been your labor of love for months. You are halfway through your slide deck. This is your shining moment. You look out to your audience, which includes the CEO, CFO, Board Members, VPs, Directors, and your leader. The next slide is the one that you <u>know</u> will tie everything together, and then you can sit back and collect your accolades. You click the advance button on the remote in your left hand, wait for the side transition to finish up, and BAM, the graph that explains everything grows from the right-hand side of the screen, bounces around the corners and lands in the middle of the slide. You are now primed and ready to accept your praise.

Something is wrong. Where are the cheers, claps, and pats on the back? What falls upon your ears is silence. There must be an emergency that pulled everyone's attention. You glance around the room to see your audience staring back at you with blank faces. Two VPs in the back corner are nodding off. Where did you go wrong?

When students are going through their schooling, they are taught the specifics of their degrees. When those students get into the workforce, they are expected to perform at the highest levels to design and execute new operations. One of the steps in the execution is being able to get buy-in from key stakeholders and communicate the idea out to the people that need to know. With businesses changing to a culture of data-driven decision making, the expectation is that all employees can analyze data and communicate the results and ideas effectively. The gap that most employees are facing is there are no formal communication classes around data presenting.

Data presentation is a combination of three things: Data Analytics, Creative Design, and Communication.

○ Data Analytics

> Data analytics is the first step of any data-driven decision making. Data analysis includes gather, clean, and prepare the data. The following information in this book will not focus much on data analytics and data analysis. Many different books are available for these subjects, from basic Excel to more advanced SQL and machine learning. The topics in this book will assume you have your data already analyzed and need to move to the next step.

○ Creative Design

> Creative design is not commonly discussed in data analytics. It is an important part and you will find in the following chapters that this book will give you a swath of ideas and instruction to make the best look for your data. Creative design can be bro-

ken down into two distinct approaches: skill and process. The creative design skill is how images, charts, graphs look and feel to the end-user. The focus is on color schemes, graphic designs, and other visual appeals. This book will give you the exact instructions down to the colors used so you can get the same look for your presentations.

○ Communication

> The most effective leaders are those that can communicate complex ideas in a straightforward way. Communication is where most people stumble. Many great ideas fail because the person cannot express their analysis concisely. Crafting a simple, understandable message will better engage the audience.

By bring three data analytics, creative design, and communication together you excel as an employee that can analyze information and be able to communicate effectively. Executives are looking for people that give them strong ideas without them having to take the time to investigate the minutia themselves. Position yourself in the company to be the expert, and people will look towards you for decision making help.

CHAPTER 2

So Fresh and So Clean

Outkast said it best, "Ain't nobody dope as me; I'm just so fresh, so clean." That is the confidence you want to have with your presentation. Too many visuals clutter your presentation, and too little visuals leave the audience guessing what message you are conveying. You want to have the freshest and cleanest presentation to share your knowledge and ideas.

Audience Confusion

Have you been an audience member in a presentation where the presenter is going on about something, but you don't know what is really being said? You are not paying attention and flipping through the hard version of the slide deck, pretending to be engaged. You eventually stumble upon a visual that looks interesting. You are not sure how to read it, so you keep flipping along. You get to the end of the handouts and start to question every decision that got you to this point, and you just want it to be over so you can go on with the rest of your day. Sound familiar?

Audience confusion is the biggest and most frequent reason for presentation failure. Executives are busy individuals with limited availability. Presenters have a small amount of time in front of key stakeholders. Those that try to fit all their knowledge into their presentation end up confusing the audience and leading to audience disengagement. This chapter will go over the research behind visual perception and how your eyes, behavior, and memory are affected. Keeping your presentation fresh and your visuals clean.

Gestalt Principles of Visual Perception

The Gestalt Principles of grouping represent the culmination of the work of early 20th-century German psychologists Max Wertheimer, Kurt Koffka, and Wolfgang Kohler. These researchers sought to understand how humans typically gain meaningful perceptions from chaotic stimuli around them. Wertheimer and company identified a set of laws addressing this natural compulsion to find order amid disorder, where the mind "informs" what the eye sees by making sense of a series of elements as an image or illusion.

Proximity

The Gestalt principle of proximity states that people tend to think of objects that are physically close together as belonging to a group. Data scientists use machine learning to group data into clusters to gain an understanding of the data. When the picture below is viewed, the audience's eyes focus on the dots as being in 3 distinct groups.

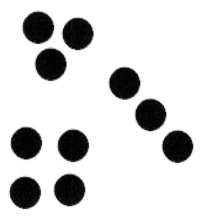

Principle Uses: When showing that a data point is more aligned with a specific group than other groups, or classifications, within the dataset. Data Scientist use clustering analysis as the main task of exploratory data mining, and a common technique for statistical data analysis.

Closure

The principle of closure states that we prefer complete shapes. Our brain will automatically fill in gaps between elements to perceive a complete image. We see the whole first. The dashes below are not connected yet we see a triangle, even though there are gaps in the image.

Principle Uses: The closure principle is used to highlight data within the figure. This principle often used unknowingly and can draw misleading or unintended conclusions. Beware not to fall into the trap of closure by looking over your visuals and make sure that data is not showing a hidden message. If you find that your visual has an unintended closure design, you can use other techniques to help the audience not see it (color, design, scaling, and positioning).

Common Region

The Common Region principal states that we group data points together if they are within a boundary. Using a line or shading can show data groupings even when data points are different shapes, sizes, or color.

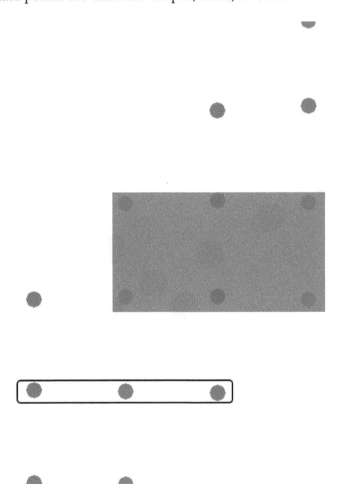

Principle Uses: Common region adds another dimension to the narrative. There are two different data sets (red and blue) with a border or shading highlighting specific sections of the dataset.

Continuation

The principle of continuation states that the human eye will identify and follow lines, curves, and sequences that are familiar. Continuation can carry between both positive and negative space. The positive space is the area/image where the data is present, the negative space is where there is no data present. Your eye wants to make connections where there is none. The graph below is not connected but you follow the dots and understand how the data is progressing.

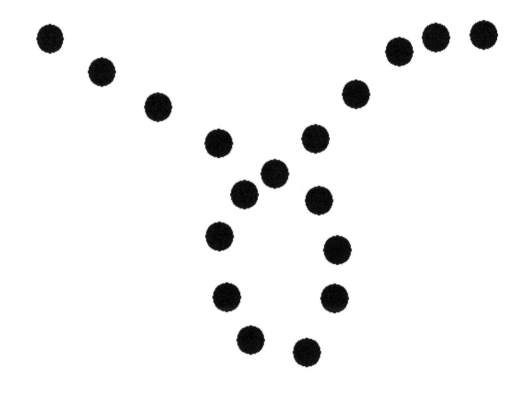

The majority of languages read left to right, so your eye follows the figure from left to right, and your brain fills in the gaps. Nothing connecting these dots, yet you see that the data is flowing from top to a loop and then back to the top. Your audience will interpret your graph without connecting the dots, which is useful for making a clean graph, but it can also be problematic. The graph below has data missing. The line shows only available data. The audience will try to fill in the gap by "connecting" the two points. Leaving the connecting up to the audience can lead to misinterpretation. Since the data is missing, there is no way to connect the two points.

Principle Uses: Understand how your audience will perceive non-connected data points and how that will affect the narrative. When continuation impedes your presentation negatively, Change the graph, visual, text to point out limitations and constraints. Give the audience tools to understand the negative space.

CHAPTER 3

Illuminate Visuals With Color: Think Like a Designer

When you started this book, you didn't expect to read about colors. Coloring your visual is an important and overlooked step. Most people use the default colors that the graph populates without a second thought. Over the years, software developers are getting better at default colors. In a pinch, the default color scheme would work, but it may not highlight your work in order to convey your message.

11

Color Basics

RGB

RGB is an abbreviation for Red, Green, and Blue. The lightwaves off of these colors can combine to make all the other colors in the visible light spectrum. The process of adding colors is best described when using a monitor, projector, or TV screen. Since the majority of presentations will be on one of these electronic device, the RGB profile will work best. Displays will keep adding colors to make the color brighter or different. White is created when all three colors are added together.

RBG is used as RGB(#,#,#), where each number can be 0 to 255. RGB(0,0,0) is black and RGB(255,255,255) is white. Since there is a maximum of 255 colors in each red, green, or blue, there can only be 16,777,216 colors in the RGB spectrum.

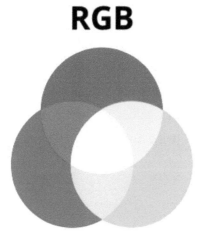

RGB

Hexadecimal Color

Hexadecimal Colors, or Web Colors, are mostly used for web development. Hexadecimal color translates the RGB color into a web-friendly color. Hexadecimal is represented by #RRGGBB with values ranging from #000000 (black) to #ffffff (white). Since Hexadecimal is a translation of RGB, there is the exact same number of colors that can be achieved by using this format.

CMYK

CMYK stands for Cyan, Magenta, Yellow, and Black. Where RGB adds colors to make different colors, CMYK does the opposite by subtracting colors. Black is the primary color and by reducing each of the color values, other colors are created. Since white is the absence of color, CMYK colors are used for physical print pieces like marketing material, flyers, cards, etc. When needing to provide hard copies of your data, utilize CMYK colors. Modern printers will make the change automatically but there maybe a slight difference between what is shown on the screen and what has been printed.

CMYK color scheme uses a percentages to determine color, such as CMYK(0%,0%,0%,0%), white, to CMYK(100%,100%,100%,100%), black. Each element of the CMYK is between 0% and 100%. Meaning there is theoretically 100,000,000 different colors in the CMYK template. Due to limitations of the human eye and printing technology, only a fraction of those colors are usable.

CMYK

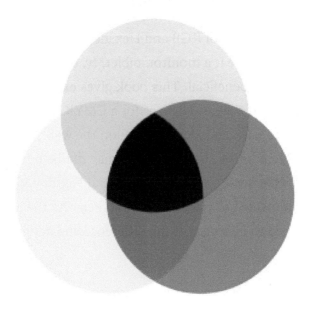

Pantone®

Pantone® standardizes the CMYK colors into groups and names. Organizations can trademark their Pantone color. Pantone color can be represented by a name (Rose Quartz) or the Pantone number (Pantone 13-1520).

This book focuses on the uses of RGB and Hexadecimal colors. With most presentations on a screen, be it a monitor, tablet, tv, or projector, these color schemes will be the most beneficial. This book gives examples of both RGB and Hexadecimal color. If the need arrises for a CMYK or Pantone color, there are conversion to RGB and Hexadecimal on the web. Since these are two different color techniques, the conversion may not be exactly accurate, but it will be close. This book mentions CMYK and Pantone if the presentation is being printed instead of projected on a screen. As the author of your presentation, you need to be aware of the difference and adjust accordingly.

Color Theory

Color theory is both the science and art of color. It explains how humans perceive color, how colors mix, match or clash, and the subliminal messages colors communicate. Color is perception and varies by person. Objects reflect light in different combinations of wavelengths. Human brains pick up on those wavelength combinations and translate them into color.

Think of the last time you were in a grocery store aisle. Take notice of the design of each of the products. What made you gravitate towards a particular product? Research has shown that color is the primary reason people buy or reject a product. This same theory applies to your audience if they can understand your presentation, buy-in to what you are presenting, and execute your recommendations.

84.7% of the total respondents think that color accounts for more than half among the various factors important for choosing products when asked to approximate the importance of color when buying products.

Source: Secretariat of the Seoul International Color Expo 2004

When used correctly, color can improve comprehension, learning, and reading. Color affects mood. Marketers have used color in advertising to increase the perception of hunger, trustworthiness, calmness, action, passion, excitement, enthusiasm, health, tranquility, wealth, success, wisdom, youthfulness, and much more. This book explores the psychology of color and how you can use it in your presentations and create compelling visuals.

Primary, Secondary, and Tertiary Colors

Primary colors are just that, the primary colors we discussed earlier of red, yellow, and blue. Secondary colors are colors that are made by mixing the primary colors that sandwich them on the color wheel. Tertiary colors are made by mixing the secondary colors that sandwich them on the color wheel.

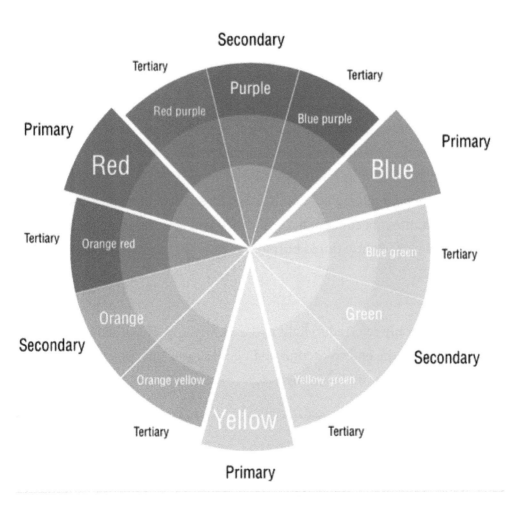

Secondary

Tertiary

Purple

Tertiary

Red purple

Blue purple

Primary

Primary

Red

Blue

Tertiary

Orange red

Blue green

Tertiary

Orange

Green

Secondary

Secondary

Orange yellow

Yellow green

Tertiary

Yellow

Tertiary

Primary

Hue

Hue is synonymous with "color." All of the primary and secondary colors, for instance, are "hues." Hues are essential when combining two primary colors to create a secondary color. Two primary colors mixed can include other tints, tones, and shades. The end color is technically more than two colors to the mixture, making your final color dependent on the compatibility of more than two colors. By mixing red and blue together, the end result is purple, but if instead, the mix contained a tent of red and a hue of blue, then the end result would be a slightly tinted purple.

Shade

Shade is commonly referred to light and dark versions of the same hue. Shade is actually the end color after adding black to a hue. Shades can vary by how much black is added to the mix.

Tint

A tint is the opposite of shade by adding white instead of black. Color can have a range of both shades and tints.

Tone

Tone sometimes referred to as saturation, is the end result when adding both white and black to a hue. Tone will be used more often for describing painting and saturation in colors being created for digital images.

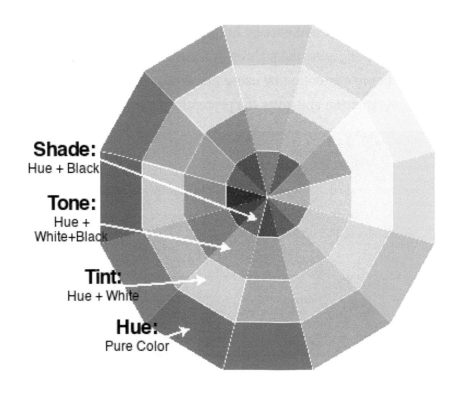

Shade:
Hue + Black

Tone:
Hue +
White+Black

Tint:
Hue + White

Hue:
Pure Color

How Color Affects Your Audience

Color impacts your audience by informing, educating, and increasing participation while engaging them through increased memory. A presenter can lose their audience's attention by using the wrong color. Color creates the mood of the presentation and gives the perception of specific characteristics.

Red

- Evokes strong emotions
- Encourages appetite
- Increases passion and intensity
- Red roses symbolize love
- Increases heart rate
- Stimulates appetite
- Creates a sense of urgency

Yellow

- Increases warmth and cheerfulness
- Stimulates mental process and nervous system
- Encourages communication
- Represents optimism and youthfulness
- Grabs attention and shows clarity
- Overuse causes eye strain and fatigue

Blue

- Associated with water and peace
- Represents calmness and serenity
- Curbs appetite
- Increases productivity
- Creates a sense of security and trust
- Communicates truth
- Most used color in office spaces
- Preferred by men

Orange

- Shows warmth
- Warns of caution
- Reflects excitement and enthusiasm
- Creates a call to action
- Shows confidence, riendliness, and cheerfulness
- Related to creativity and pleasure

Green

- Demonstrates health and tranquillity
- Denotes nature
- Symbolizes money and growth
- Associates with wealth and growth
- Relaxing, non-threatening message
- Human eye sensitivity can easily discern differences in shade

Purple

- Shows royalty, wealth, success and wisdom
- Soothe and calm
- Represents creativity and imagination

Color Schemes

The combination of colors in a presentation is the color scheme. The color scheme will define the presentation by the emotions the colors inflict, as described above, and they also brand the presenter and the presentation. A defined color scheme should be carried through to all presentations. The audience will get the know the look and feel of the visuals and will help the flow of the presentation. This section will cover the basics of creating a color scheme and then give a few examples. Feel free to use the examples or take the journey in designing your own. Once you have defined what your brand will look like, keep it as a template for future presentations.

Color schemes for data presentations include:

- Complementary Color

- Analogous Color

- Triadic Color

- Monochromatic Color

Complementary Color Schemes

Complementary colors are opposites on the color wheel, red and green, for example. Because there's a sharp contrast between the two colors, they can really make imagery pop, but overusing them can create audience fatigue. Using a complementary color scheme in your presentation offers sharp contrast and clear differentiation between visuals.

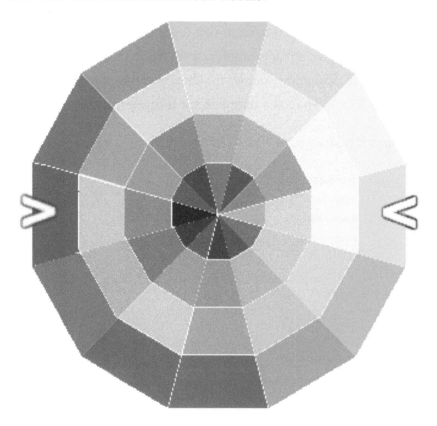

Analogous Color Schemes

Analogous colors sit next to one another on the color wheel. When creating an analogous color scheme, one color will dominate, one will support, and another will accent. In presentation visuals, analogous color schemes are not only pleasing to the eye but can effectively instruct the audience how to take action.

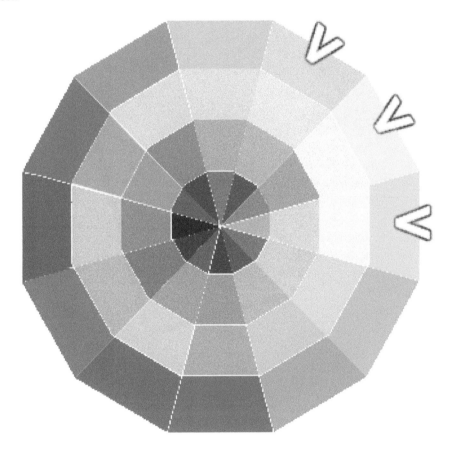

Triadic Color Schemes

Triadic colors are evenly spaced around the color wheel and tend to be very bright and dynamic. Using a triadic color scheme in a presentation creates visual contrast and harmony simultaneously, making each item stand out while making the overall presentation pop.

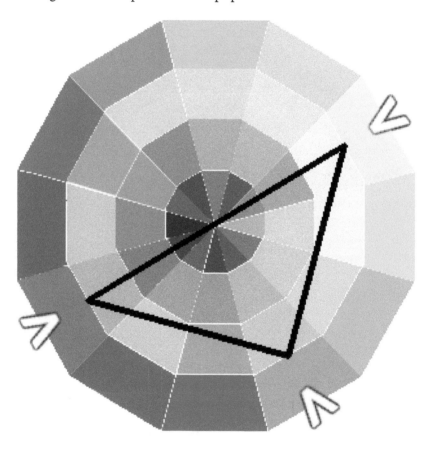

Monochromatic Color Schemes

Monochromatic colors are all the different tints, tones, and shades in the same hue family, the easiest and most effective way to use a color scheme. Most presentation softwares already have this type of color scheme built-in. The main color, or hue, is the primary color, the shade is the secondary color, and the tint is the accent color.

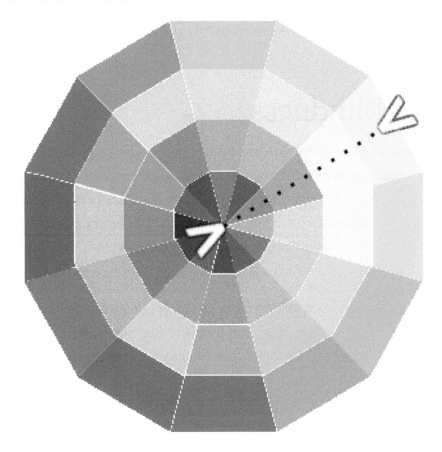

60-30-10 Rule

60-30-10 rule has been used to describe color and space balance for interior design to marketing. For presentations, the 60-30-10 rule states that 60% of visuals should be the primary color, 30% should be the secondary color, and 10% should be the accent color. When designing a color scheme to define your brand, use the 60-30-10 rule to avoid overusing colors and space. Anytime the is audience bombarded with unruly visuals, the presenter will lose their engagement.

Color Blindness

Know your audience. If there is someone in your audience is color blind, adjust accordingly. While color can add depth to graphs, lack of color can make graphs illegible. Have you received a hard copy of a presentation that was copied in black and white? You are expected to interpret a chart with shades of gray. This is similar to people with color blindness. The details are lost.

Color schemes that include blue/yellow or red/green are on opposite sides of the color wheel but are very similar in intensity. Keeping colors that contrast in lightness is better for color-blind individuals as well as making black and white copies.

Selecting Effective Colors

- **Black Font/Light Background (or visa versa):** Use high contrast of black text on a light background or white text on a dark background.

- **Label The Chart Elements:** A legend that relies only on color is hard for all viewers, not just colorblind individuals. Label each data element directly on the chart.

- **High Contrast Data Values:** Using different colors for each data point can help tell the story. Ensure that the colors used are contrasting. Because it is easier for the eyes to decipher lightness to darkness use a single color with different shades for each of the data points.

- **Gray Scale:** When in doubt, change to grayscale and see how it holds up. Print the whole thing in black and white to verify all of the details are coming through.

Color Scheme Examples

#AFC97E	#EDFF86	#877B66	#153B3D	#E0D2C3
#BEB8EB	#618985	#414535	#F2E3BC	#C19875
#5BC0EB	#FDE74C	#E26D5C	#9BC53D	#FA7921
#F3E8EE	#BACDB0	#A39171	#475B63	#2E2C2F
#157F1F	#EEEEEE	#FFF8F0	#131515	#2B2C28
#044389	#FCFF4B	#FFAD05	#7CAFC4	#5995ED

CHAPTER 4

Determine the Most Effective Visual

"What graph should I choose?" is a question that should be asked prior to starting the presentation, and if often overlooked. You have minimal time with a specific captive audience. Talk about high stakes. The way you showcase your ideas is as important as the presentation. A presentation's tone and success is set by the visuals used. A good first impression applies to every visual in your presentation because it will be the first time your audience has seen each visual.

Effective Visuals

Doing a simple internet search shows that there are over 150+ different visuals available to present an array of different types of datasets. In the best conditions, research has found that a presenter has 20 - 40 seconds to make a positive impact on your audience and keep them engaged. Technology is your enemy keeping executives and key stakeholders in contact with the outside world. Your goal is to keep your audience engaged and transfer your knowledge to them so they can provide support and input. Having confusing and ineffective visuals creates an environment where your captive audience starts to think about other things, and then the "Technology Creep" will happen.

Technology Creep is the slow and steady disengagement from the audience due to the distraction of technology. It happens slowly and is very contagious. It starts with one executive being distracted. That one instance changes the disposition of the meeting where others begin to become aware of the outside world through their devices. With phones, watches, computers, and tablets, you cannot remove the distractions. Your presentation will have to be capable of keeping your stakeholders and executives capitative with the information you have to share with them.

Choosing A Graph

Distribution

Arranging data into the frequency of occurrences or natural ranges. The reader of the chart will realize how many in each category.

Composition

Composition is the process of combining distinct parts, elements, categories, or processes into one visual. Helping the view understand how such parts are related.

Composition

TIME

Few Periods

Relative
Differences

100%
Stacked
Column Chart

Absolute
Differences

Stacked
Column Chart

Many Periods

Relative
Differences

100%
Stacked Area
Chart

Absolute
Differences

Stacked Area
Chart

STATIC

Piece Of A
Total

Pie Chart

Changes By
Category

Waterfall
Chart

Relationship

Showing how categories are related. Helps the viewer compare the connection or association between each category.

Relationship

Two Variables

Scatter Chart

Three Variables

Bubble Chart

Comparison

Using time or categories, the audience can compare from data point to data point. Time (seconds, minutes, hours, days, weeks, months, quarters, years) can show seasonal or non-seasonal trends. Categorical graphs will show trends between different categories.

Comparison

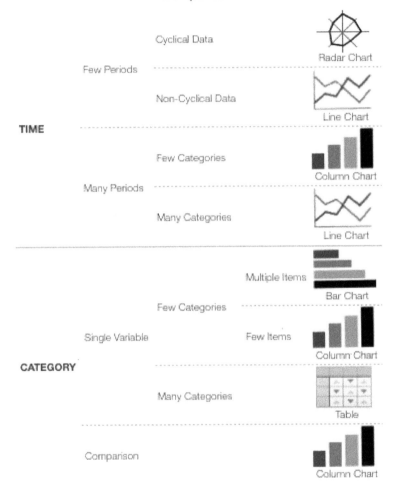

TIME

Few Periods
- Cyclical Data — Radar Chart
- Non-Cyclical Data — Line Chart

Many Periods
- Few Categories — Column Chart
- Many Categories — Line Chart

CATEGORY

Single Variable
- Few Categories
  - Multiple Items — Bar Chart
  - Few Items — Column Chart
- Many Categories — Table

Comparison — Column Chart

You Are The Expert

You did the work, shifted through raw unmanaged data, put hours in understanding the situation and background, you researched the most appropriate course of action, and devised a recommendation. You put all of this into a condensed presentation. You have the knowledge and are the expert in this aspect. It can take weeks, months, or years to get the chance to make your case. After all the time and work you put into crafting your message and polishing your presentation, maximize the impact on your audience. Keep the presentation to two-thirds of the allotted time and use the other third for questions and discussion at the end. An excellent presentation will lead to discussion, questions, and actionable next steps.

When making the presentation, you want to show you are the expert about the topic at hand. Give your audience enough information and let them make their own conclusions. You want your audience to ask questions. With compelling visuals, you can steer the discussion into a direction that you envisioned. Presenting all the information at once creates an environment of "analysis paralysis" where over-analyzing or over-thinking a situation can lead to no action or solution.

You are the expert, and executives look to you for guidance. They want and value your input to help them with decision making. They look to you for your knowledge and trust your insight. This can only happen if they trust you, and they believe what you are presenting. The visuals and graphs that you choose create opportunities to build on that trust. You are the expert. Experts know when and how to use each visual. Take an extra moment to make sure you are choosing the correct graph to display the data that leads to the actionable steps you want.

Simple Text

Sometimes a simple text or number is all that is needed to make an impact. Most single data sourced charts can be changed into a simple text. A graph takes time for the audience to get acquainted and to be able to comprehend, where simple text can be read and understood clearly. The graph below shows the student loan debt from the first quarter in 2003 through the last quarter of 2018.

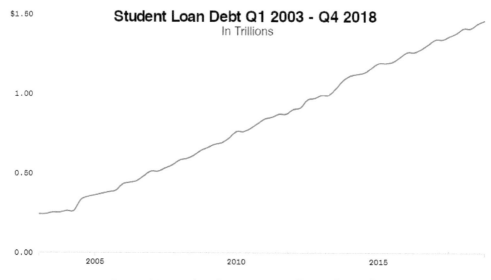

Source: New York Fed Consumer Credit Panel, Equifax

As an audience member, it is challenging to grasp the impact of this type of visual. The gist is that student loan debt is growing, but the audience does not see specifics. Does the audience know what Q1 2003 and Q4 2018 represent? The reader may be confused by the above graph. There are no data labels to explicitly state in the past 16 years how much student loan debt has grown. The estimation is the chart starts around $250 million and goes to $1.5 trillion. The numbers are so big that they are hard to grasp. A percentage would be easier to understand, but the audience is left to calculate that themselves. Below is a simple text that can be better understood.

508%

Increase in student loan debt in sixteen years. From the first quareter of 2003 at $240 million to the last quarter of 2018 at $1.24 trillion.
Source: New York Fed Consumer Credit Panel, Equifax

The above visual grabs your attention and is more dramatic than the previous chart. With a significant number, the audience can read the visual and understand it easier than deciphering a line chart. The orange color warns of caution and urgency. The bolded parts of the accompanying paragraph make important information stand out. The audience can get information quickly without the presenter having to explain or orientate the audience. Leaving more time to discuss the ideas instead of explaining single visuals.

Focusing the audience

When using text as a visual, the presenter must focus the audience's attention on pertinent parts. All the information in the text is important and supports the main idea, but the main idea can get lost in the text. For example, how many 6's are in the visual below?

6633779405732220 3545
3871900980702064 5674
2960969286689730 1392

The correct number is eight. As an audience member, it is challenging to find the critical information (6's for this example). There are no visual cues to help the audience reach a conclusion. The presenter is asking the audience to "hunt" for the answer and will eventually lead to audience disengagement. The visual below helps the audience by changing the text to make the critical information jump out.

66337794057322203545
38719009807020645674
29609692866897301392

It is easier now to count the number of 6's because the font is different. This book will go into seven different ways to focus the audience's attention for a simple text visual.

Bold

The space race was a series of competitive technology demonstrations between the United States and the Soviet Union, **aiming to show superiority in spaceflight.** It was an outgrowth of the mid-20th-century Cold War, a tense global conflict that pitted the ideologies of capitalism and communism against one another.

Color

The space race was a series of competitive technology demonstrations between the United States and the Soviet Union, aiming to show superiority in spaceflight. It was an outgrowth of the mid-20th-century Cold War, a tense global conflict that pitted the ideologies of capitalism and communism against one another.

Italics

The space race was a series of competitive technology demonstrations between the United States and the Soviet Union, aiming *to show superiority in spaceflight.* It was an outgrowth of the mid-20th-century Cold War, a tense global conflict that pitted the ideologies of capitalism and communism against one another.

Size

The space race was a series of competitive technology demonstrations between the United States and the Soviet Union, aiming to show superiority in

spaceflight. It was an outgrowth of the mid-20th-century Cold War,

a tense global conflict that pitted the ideologies of capitalism and communism against one another.

White Space

The space race was a series of competitive technology demonstrations between the United States and the Soviet Union,

aiming to show superiority in spaceflight.

It was an outgrowth of the mid-20th-century Cold War, a tense global conflict that pitted the ideologies of capitalism and communism against one another.

Underline

The space race was a series of competitive technology demonstrations be-tween the United States and the Soviet Union, aiming to show superiority in spaceflight. It was an <u>outgrowth of the mid-20th-century Cold War</u>, a tense global conflict that pitted the ideologies of capitalism and communism against one another.

Enclosure

The space race was a series of competitive technology demonstrations be-tween the United States and the Soviet Union, aiming to show superiority in spaceflight. It was an outgrowth of the mid-20th-century Cold War, a tense global conflict that pitted the ideologies of capitalism and communism against one another.

Font

Font selection is critical. Some fonts convey whimsy that may not need to be in a presentation, while other fonts may be hard to read at a distance. The incorrect font can lead to audience disengagement. Things to avoid:

- Condensed font.

- *Using Bold and Italic simultaneously*

- ALL CAPS

- White Text, Black Background

- *Stylized Fonts*

- T r a c k i n g

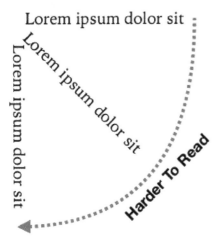

Harder To Read

Lorem ipsum dolor sit amet, consectetur adipiscing elit.
Lorem ipsum dolor sit amet, consectetur adipiscing elit.
Lorem ipsum dolor sit amet, consectetur adipiscing elit.
Lorem ipsum dolor sit amet, consectetur adipiscing elit.
LOREM IPSUM DOLOR SIT AMET, CONSECTETUR ADIPISCING ELIT.

Lorem ipsum dolor sit amet, consectetur adipiscing elit.

Lorem ipsum dolor sit

Lorem ipsum dolor sit

Lorem ipsum dolor sit

Harder To Read

Keeping font to the basic Serif and San-serif font family will help with the readability of the visual. The fonts in this book use Iowan Old Style, Helvetica, Helvetica Neue. Others to consider are Courier, Georgia, and the standard Times New Roman. Test out fonts and find one that will work thought the whole presentation. Using too many fonts will distract the viewer.

Tables & Heat Maps

Tables

Tables are a visual snapshot of data. If your audience needs to understand the numbers use a table instead of a graph. A graph with large amounts of data needs to be explained to the audience, where a table is easy to read, and the presenter does not need to take time orientating the audience to the graph. Tables in presentations can be challenging to understand. Make sure there isn't too much information in the tables that creates clutter. If you want to present the idea while showing supporting data, the table should be a handout so the audience can still listen to the presenter as well as understand the numbers. The table still needs the same attention as the presentation, even if the table is not in the presentation. Tables not created correctly leads to more questions for the audience, and the presenter will lose time and engagement.

Tables can include visuals like a line or bar graph within the cells, which can aid in communicating ideas.

City	Units Sold
Springfield	384
Clinton	378
Madison	286
Arlington	270
Franklin	264
Washington	210
Salem	190
Fairfield	133
Chester	105

Heat Maps

Heat maps add another layer of information by using visual cues. A heat map is a table with colored cells or text that allows the audience's eyes to quickly find the vital information. In the table below, it is difficult to find the most essential information, all the data looks similar. By adding a visual cue to the table and creating a heat map, the viewer can easily find that Company D has the highest percentage.

Table

	CATEGORY 1	CATEGORY 2	CATEGORY 3	CATEGORY 4
COMPANY A	27.69%	82.47%	48.59%	56.76%
COMPANY B	49.63%	27.16%	70.16%	17.11%
COMPANY C	49.94%	74.18%	82.76%	22.39%
COMPANY D	56.35%	68.59%	94.37%	11.65%
COMPANY E	14.80%	15.43%	33.70%	41.59%

Heat Map

	CATEGORY 1	CATEGORY 2	CATEGORY 3	CATEGORY 4
COMPANY A	27.69%	82.47%	48.59%	56.76%
COMPANY B	49.63%	27.16%	70.16%	
COMPANY C	49.94%	74.18%	82.76%	22.39%
COMPANY D	56.35%	68.59%	94.37%	
COMPANY E			33.70%	41.59%

Reduce mental processing power that the audience has to exert to understand the presenter's point. As stated earlier in the color section, shades of green are easiest to decipher by the human eye. Most heat maps are colored from red to green or from light red to dark red, which is harder on the audience's eyes. Using different shades of green is pleasing to the eyes, and it is easier to pick out the most crucial information. Also, reducing the font color helps the viewer find information quickly.

Styling

There are some rules to make your graph visually pleasing and understandable, like font, number and text alignment, colors, ordering, and borders.

Numbers

• Align whole numbers flush right

Whole Numbers Aligned Left	
City	Units Sold
Springfield	10000
Clinton	1000
Madison	100
Arlington	10
Franklin	1

Whole Numbers Aligned Right	
City	Units Sold
Springfield	10000
Clinton	1000
Madison	100
Arlington	10
Franklin	1

• Align decimal numbers on the decimal point

Decimal Flush Left

City	Efficiency
Springfield	10.18
Clinton	9.49
Madison	8
Arlington	7.40
Franklin	.23

Decimal Flush Right

City	Efficiency
Springfield	10.18
Clinton	9.49
Madison	8
Arlington	7.40
Franklin	.23

Centered on Decimal

City	Efficiency
Springfield	10.18
Clinton	9.49
Madison	8.00
Arlington	7.40
Franklin	0.23

• Display the unit only once

Unit Display Incorrect

City	Sales
Springfield	$11,382,528.00
Franklin	$7,010,784.00
Arlington	$6,974,910.00
Washington	$5,918,000.00
Clinton	$5,352,858.00
Madison	$3,897,894.00

Unit Display Correct

City	Sales (Millions)
Springfield	$11.38M
Franklin	7.01
Arlington	6.97
Washington	5.92
Clinton	5.35
Madison	3.90

Ordering & Sorting

• Present tables with multiple data points vertically.

Comparative Data Horizontally

	Springfield	Clinton	Madison	Arlington	Franklin	Washington
Salespeople	12	14	13	10	8	11
Units Sold	384	378	286	270	264	210
Total Sales	$11.38M	5.35	3.90	6.97	7.01	5.92

Comparative Data Vertically

City	Salespeople	Units Sold	Total Sales
Springfield	12	384	$11.38M
Clinton	14	378	5.35
Madison	13	286	3.90
Arlington	10	270	6.97
Franklin	8	264	7.01
Washington	11	210	5.92

• Order the table logically either alphabetical or by values

Random Entries			Sorted Alphabetically			Sorted by Values	
City	**Sales (Millions)**		**City**	**Sales (Millions)**		**City**	**Sales (Millions)**
Springfield	$11.38M		Arlington	$6.97M		Springfield	$11.38M
Clinton	5.35		Clinton	5.35		Franklin	7.01
Madison	3.90		Franklin	7.01		Arlington	6.97
Arlington	6.97		Madison	3.90		Washington	5.92
Franklin	7.01		Springfield	11.38		Clinton	5.35
Washington	5.92		Washington	5.92		Madison	3.90

Gridlines & Shading

- Remove any unhelpful gridlines. Large tables with multiple data points are busy, removing any unhelpful gridlines cleans up the table for the viewer to read easily.

Unhelpful Borders

City	Salespeople	Units Sold	Total Sales
Springfield	12	384	$11.38M
Clinton	14	378	5.35
Madison	13	286	3.90
Arlington	10	270	6.97
Franklin	8	264	7.01
Washington	11	210	5.92

Unhelpful Gridlines

City	Salespeople	Units Sold	Total Sales
Springfield		12	384	$11.38M
Clinton		14	378	5.35
Madison		13	286	3.90
Arlington		10	270	6.97
Franklin		8	264	7.01
Washington		11	210	5.92

Unhelpful Shading

City	Salespeople	Units Sold	Total Sales
Springfield	12	384	$11.38M
Clinton	14	378	5.35
Madison	13	286	3.90
Arlington	10	270	6.97
Franklin	8	264	7.01
Washington	11	210	5.92

• Add only visual cues that help the view understand the table. Shade only the important column and break up the data by natural grouping or every three lines.

Helpful Table

City	Salespeople	Units Sold	Total Sales
Springfield	12	384	$11.38M
Clinton	14	378	5.35
Madison	13	286	3.90
Arlington	10	270	6.97
Franklin	8	264	7.01
Washington	11	210	5.92

Graphs and Charts

Line Graph

Line graphs shows trends of single or multiple data series over time. The x-axis of the graph will represent time, and the y-axis will represent values. Ensuring that the axis distances are the same, limits the chances of skewing. When showing a line graph with multiple series of data, highlight the main series with a bold, primary color and muted secondary color for the rest of the series. Monochromatic color schemes works best when graphing multiple series.

Styling

- **Y-Axis Height:** Changing the y-axis scale can skew the trend to show too flat or too exaggerated. Chose a y-axis scale that shows two-thirds of the chart area. The scale should also display important data points that will help determine the rage.

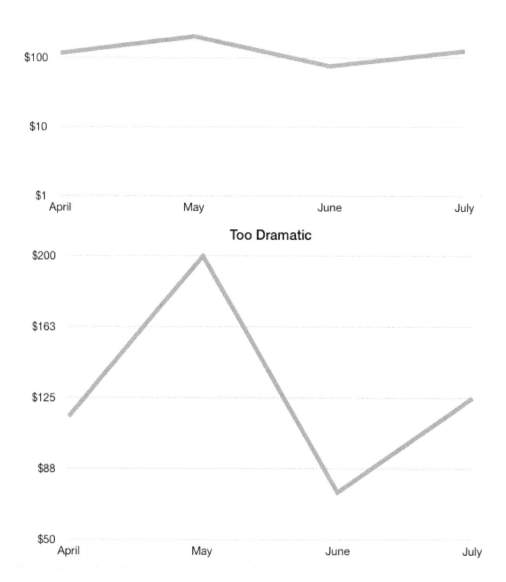

Too Flat

$100

$10

$1

April　　　　　May　　　　　June　　　　　July

Too Dramatic

$200

$163

$125

$88

$50

April　　　　　May　　　　　June　　　　　July

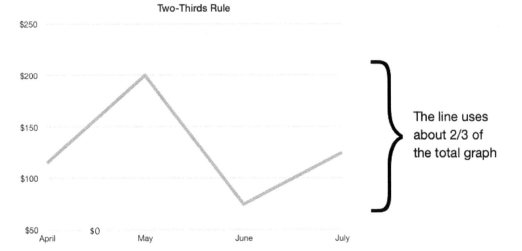

Two-Thirds Rule

$250

$200

$150

$100

$50 $0
April   May   June   July

The line uses about 2/3 of the total graph

- **Y-Axis Increments:** Using non-natural increments along the y-axis is difficult to understand. Natural increments are more straightforward for the audience to recognize the data between to points.

Natural Increments	Non-Natural Increments
0, 1, 2, 3, 4, 5...	1, 2, 3, 4, 5...
0, 2, 4, 6, 8, 10...	0, 3, 6, 9, 12...
0, 5, 10, 15, 20...	0, 4, 8, 12, 16...
0, 10, 20, 30, 40...	0, 8, 16, 24, 32...
0, 25, 50, 75, 100...	0, 12, 24, 36...
0%, 20%, 40%, 60%...	0, 15, 30, 45...
0, 0.25, 0.50, 0.75...	0%, 6%, 12%, 18%...

Non-Natural Increments

Natural Increments

58

- **Zero Baseline:** When the data does not start at 0, make sure to include a zero baseline and avoid the y-axis with values close to 0. Increasing the y-axis to start at zero gives the audience a frame of reference.

Non-Zero Baseline

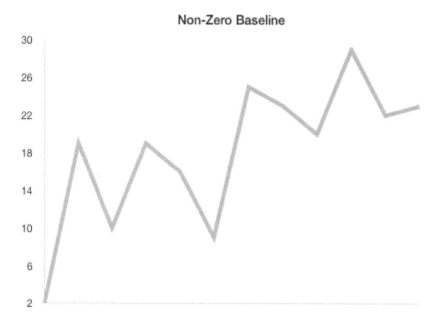

Zero Baseline

- **Line Weight:** Line charts show data over time, which can include massive amounts of data. Think about the stock market and how every second, the price of the stock changes. All those price changes are data points. A line that is too thin will fade into the background, and hard to read, a line that is too thick will not show important twists and turns of the data.

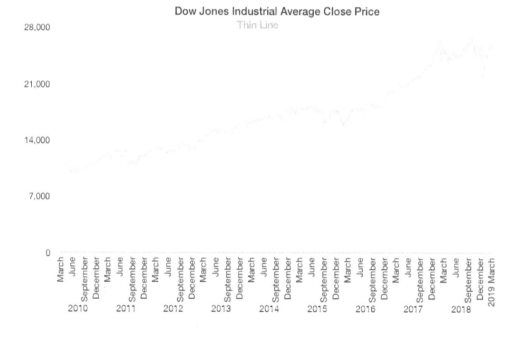

Dow Jones Industrial Average Close Price

Thin Line

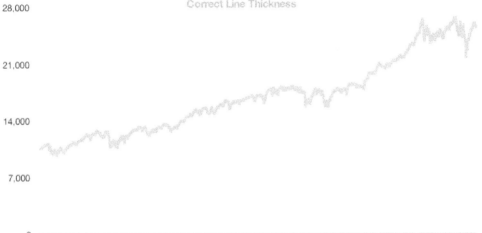

Dow Jones Industrial Average Close Price

Correct Line Thickness

• **Labeling**: When using more than one data series, add the labeling directly on the graph

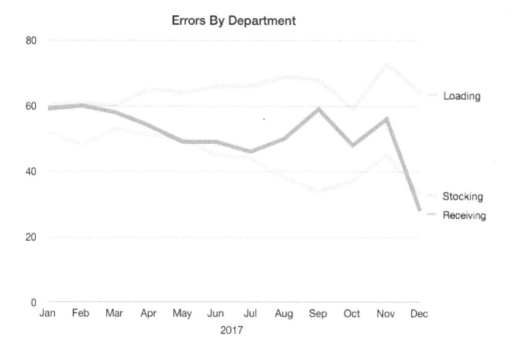

• **Four, No More:** In a single chart, keep the maximum to four data series. More than four starts to confuse the audience and muddle the point of the graph. The purpose of the line chart is to compare data series over time, if more than four are needed, use a panel series for the charts. In a panel series, the y-axis data labels only need to be on the first graph of each row. All graphs need to have the same min and max for the y-axis.

Too Busy

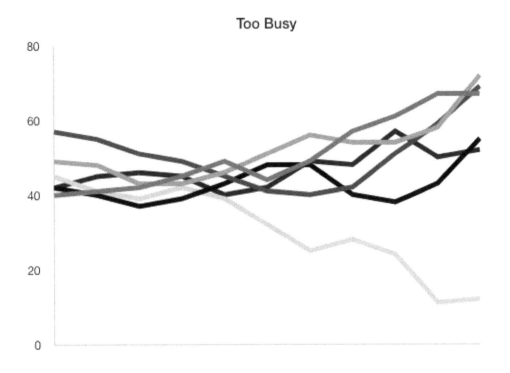

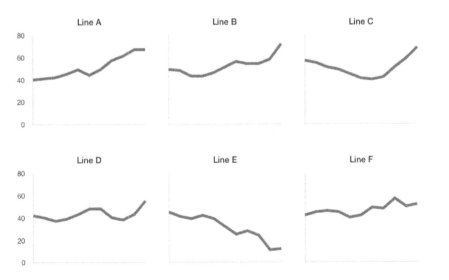

Line A

Line B

Line C

Line D

Line E

Line F

• **Forecasting:** When using a line chart to show forecast data, change the forecasted section to highlight the information. Making the line a different style (color, stroke, or weight) and shading the chart area to highlight the data.

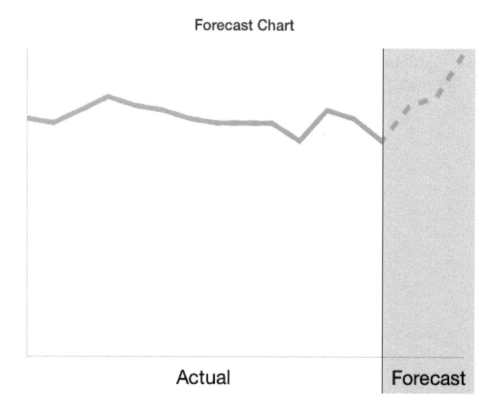

Forecast Chart

Actual | Forecast

Scatter Plot

Scatter plots are great to show 1-3 data series against two variables. Scatterplots are great to show relationships between the two variables. Scatterplots do not use category axis, both x and y-axis are numerical.

Styling

- **Simple Points:** Data points are best understood if they are stylized to be related to a brand or dramatically different. Similar data styling is hard to spot the differences.

- **Text & Coloring:** When plotting the data series, maximize the idea by adding text and changing color to show vital information.

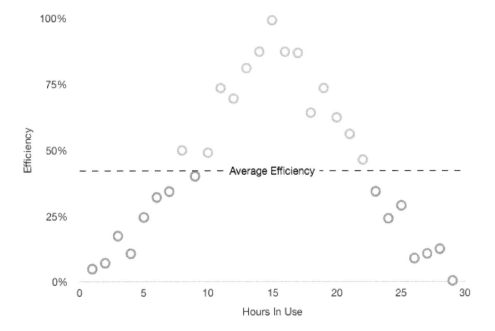

-

- **Limit The Number Of Data Series:** Scatter plots give lots of information at a single graph, and too many data series can convolute the overall message. Keep the total number of data series and data points to a minimum, 3 data series at the max. More than 3 data series creates a convoluted graph that most people will have trouble understanding.

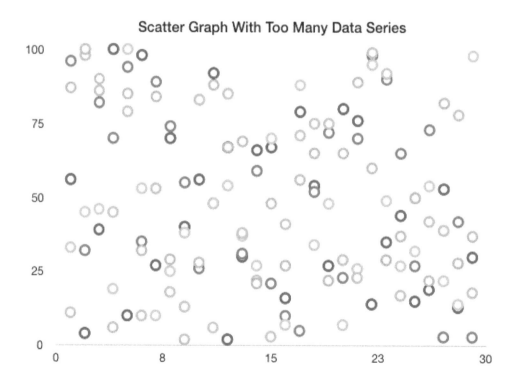

Scatter Graph With Too Many Data Series

Bubble Chart

Bubble charts, similar to scatter graphs, plot data in relation to the x and y-axis. Bubble charts add a third dimension to the graphs by the size of the data point. This third relationship can show volume, or size, of the data point represented (number of participants, cash flow, market share, any numerical value). Also, like scatter graphs, bubble charts use numerical axis and not categorical.

Styling

- **Consistent Color**: To create a proper bubble chart, sometimes that requires adding multiple data series, and charts will graph those as different colors. Stay with one color the whole chart. Various colors distract the audience.

- **Labeling**: Label directly on the chart. Labeling the series name and the bubble value helps the audience get an understanding of what is going on in the graph. Keep the labeling simple and to a minimum. If the value of the bubble is substantial then truncate the number by using thousands, millions, or billions.

- **Key**: Add a key that shows what the bubble size represents. Most presenters skip this part, and the audience does not know what the graph is stating.

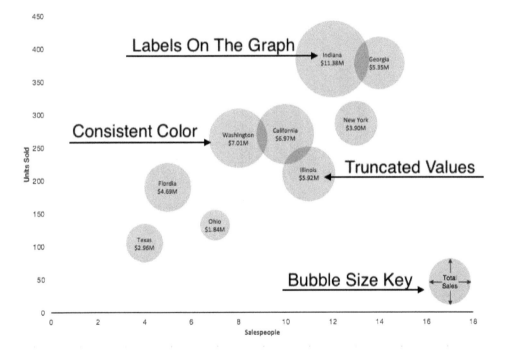

Horizontal Bar Graph

Contrary to popular belief, horizontal and vertical bar charts are not interchangeable. Depending on the number of variables needed to be presented, a vertical graph may not be the best option. Use a horizontal bar graph when the category labels are anything other than horizontal. Text that is at an angle or vertical is harder to read.

Hard To Read

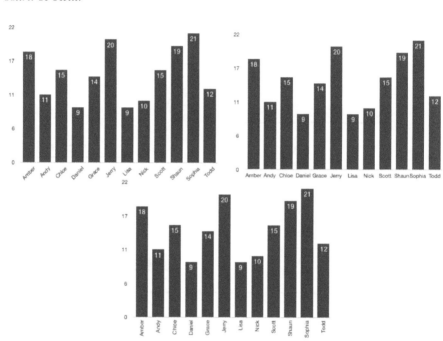

Easy To Read

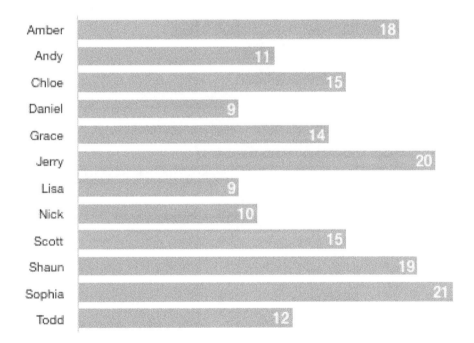

Name	Value
Amber	18
Andy	11
Chloe	15
Daniel	9
Grace	14
Jerry	20
Lisa	9
Nick	10
Scott	15
Shaun	19
Sophia	21
Todd	12

Styling

• **Order:** Plot horizontal bars ranking by bar size or alphabetical order. When plotting horizontal bars over time, the most recent data should be at the top of the graph.

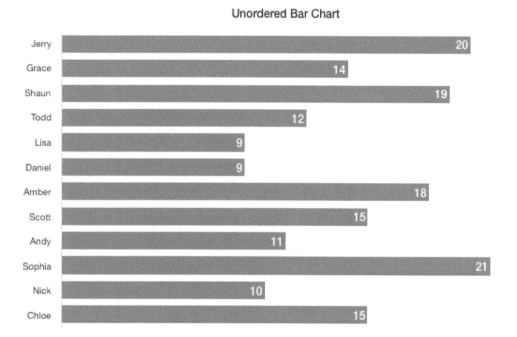

Ranked Bar Chart

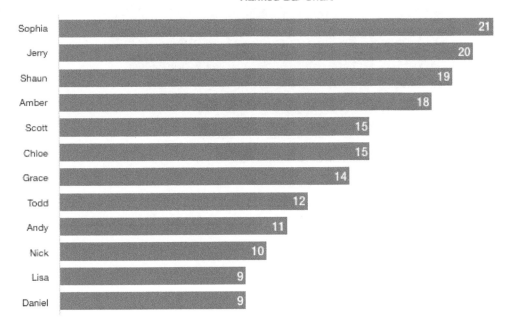

Sophia	21
Jerry	20
Shaun	19
Amber	18
Scott	15
Chloe	15
Grace	14
Todd	12
Andy	11
Nick	10
Lisa	9
Daniel	9

- **Lines:** Remove lines, grids, scales, and horizontal axis. These graph elements create clutter and confusion. Visual comparison of the different bar lengths is hard to measure and evaluate the impact. Removing the clutter and adding data labels directly on the graph will help the audience understand the information.

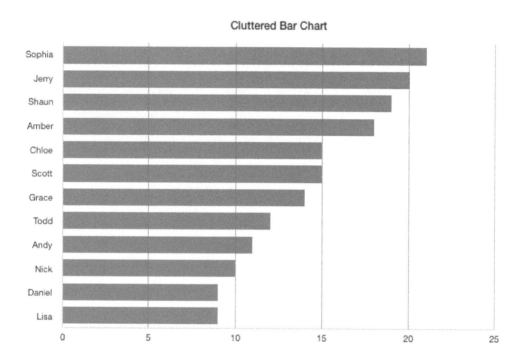

Cluttered Bar Chart

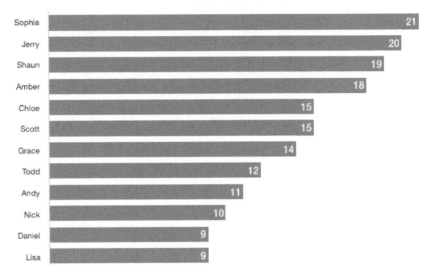

Uncluttered Bar Chart

- **Negative Bars:** Bars to the left of the y-axis represent negative numbers, bars to the right of the y-axis represents positive numbers. If the dataset contains multiple negative numbers, a vertical graph creates a more striking image. When graphing both positive and negative numbers, the negative bars can be shaded differently.

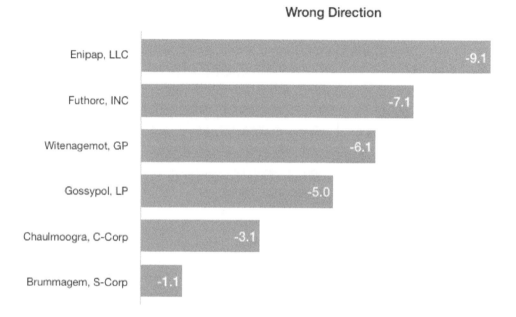

Wrong Direction

Enipap, LLC	-9.1
Futhorc, INC	-7.1
Witenagemot, GP	-6.1
Gossypol, LP	-5.0
Chaulmoogra, C-Corp	-3.1
Brummagem, S-Corp	-1.1

Correct Direction

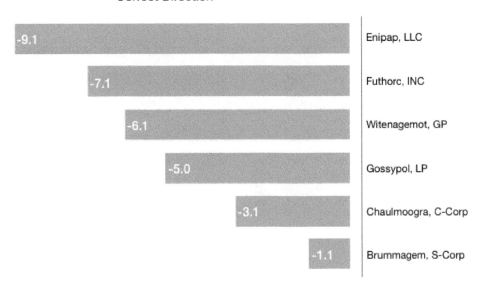

-9.1	Enipap, LLC
-7.1	Futhorc, INC
-6.1	Witenagemot, GP
-5.0	Gossypol, LP
-3.1	Chaulmoogra, C-Corp
-1.1	Brummagem, S-Corp

Mixing Positive and Negative Numbers

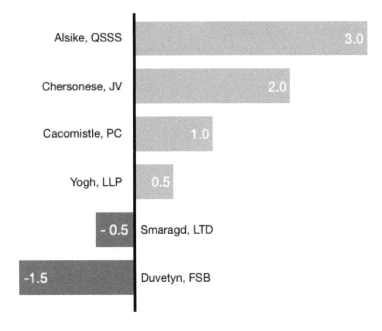

Alsike, QSSS	3.0
Chersonese, JV	2.0
Cacomistle, PC	1.0
Yogh, LLP	0.5
-0.5	Smaragd, LTD
-1.5	Duvetyn, FSB

- **Long Lists**: Long lists can be broken up by a thin line in groups of five to help the audience read the graph.

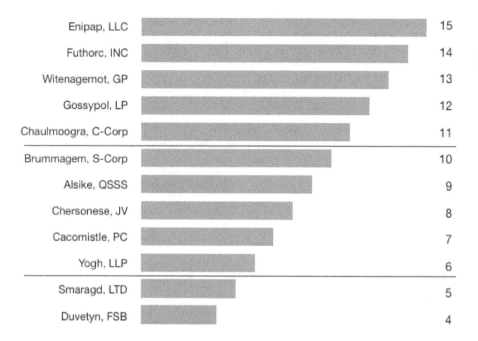

Enipap, LLC	15
Futhorc, INC	14
Witenagemot, GP	13
Gossypol, LP	12
Chaulmoogra, C-Corp	11
Brummagem, S-Corp	10
Alsike, QSSS	9
Chersonese, JV	8
Cacomistle, PC	7
Yogh, LLP	6
Smaragd, LTD	5
Duvetyn, FSB	4

Vertical Bar Graph

Vertical bar graphs show a comparison from category to category and data point to data point. It is easy to clutter up vertical bar graphs with multiple series. Keep these graphs clean and simple. Vertical bar graphs are the simplest visual for the audience, and the goal is to let the graph stand on its own. The audience will get confused if there is too much going on, and the presenter can limit confusion by breaking out the data into multiple graphs.

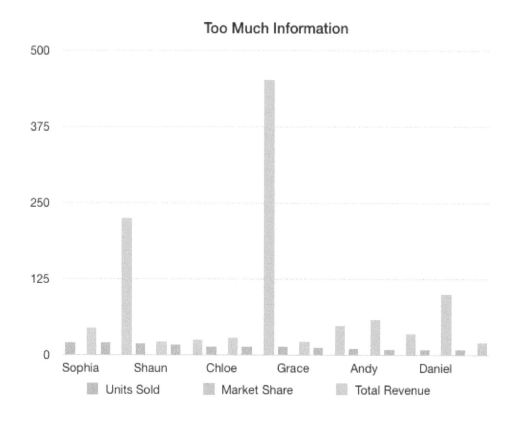

Too Much Information

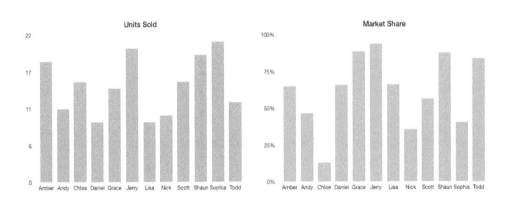

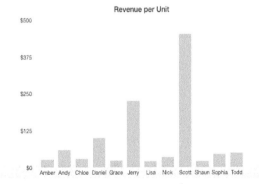

Styling

- **Bar Spacing:** Keeping the bars twice the width of the spaces. To narrow or too wide are not visually appealing and can lead to audience disengagement.

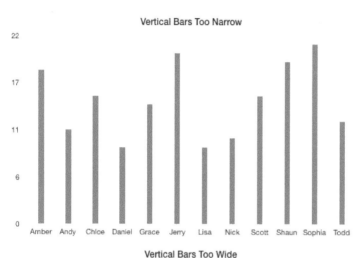

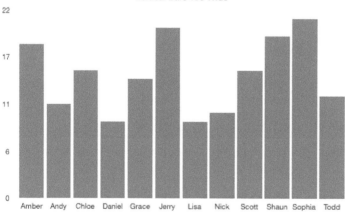

- **Shading and Textures:** Shading and textures are distracting to the viewer. Keep the colors simple and avoid distractions.

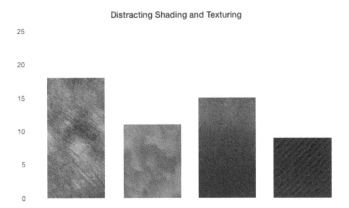

Distracting Shading and Texturing

- **3D and Shadows:** *DO NOT USE.* Creating 3D graphs or adding shading will leave the audience guessing where the top of the bar meets the graph.

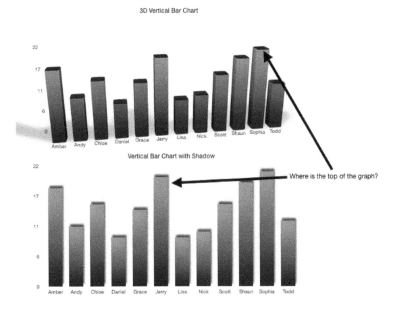

3D Vertical Bar Chart

Vertical Bar Chart with Shadow

Where is the top of the graph?

- **Projected Data:** When a graph needs to include data that is projected or estimated, change the data series to a lighter color within the color pallet of the presentation theme and label as needed.

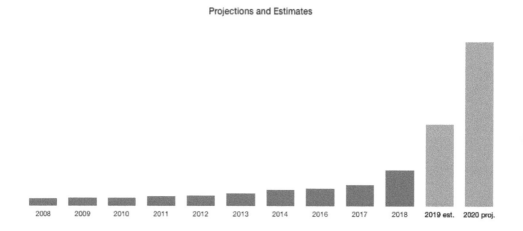

-

- **Starting at 0:** Truncating graphs leads to confusion and misrepresentation of the data. Smart audience members will question what the presenter is trying to hide by truncating the data. The presenter will be meet with inquisition rather than trust.

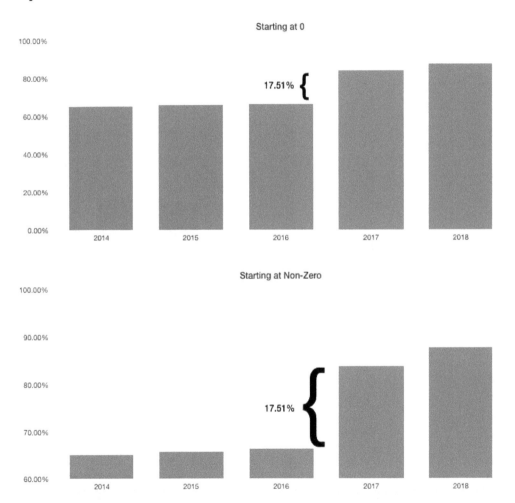

- **Negative Numbers:** Some presenters show negative numbers by changing the color of the data point to a red color. By showing negative numbers this way, it leads to a "zebra" graph leading to contrasting colors. Keep the data series the same but shade the negative part of the graph.

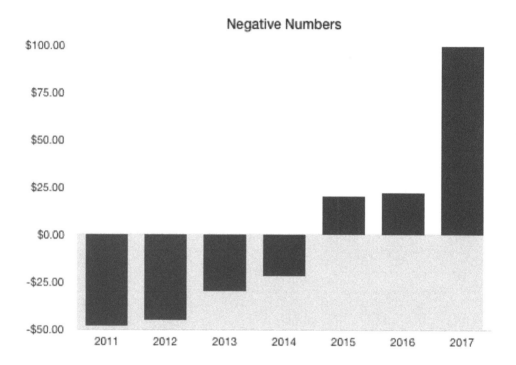

• **Story Telling:** The graph needs to stand on its own and tell a story without any help from the presenter. The data points might be more effective if they showed changes.

YEAR	MARKET SHARE	PERCENT CHANGE
2011	83.86%	
2012	70.55%	-13.31%
2013	52.95%	-17.60%
2014	67.66%	14.71%
2015	66.35%	-1.31%
2016	78.33%	11.98%
2017	65.79%	-12.54%
2018	73.60%	7.81%

Market Share

Market Share Change

Waterfall Chart

Waterfall charts are great at showing categorical variations. The groupings can be quantitative, i.e., year over year revenue, or by categories, i.e., contracts sent vs. contracts signed. Waterfall charts are a great storytelling tool to show the effectiveness of a process or growth.

Styling

- **Simple Labels:** When using waterfall charts to show a process, keep the chart labels simple. Wordy labels will just distract from the story the presenter is trying to convey.

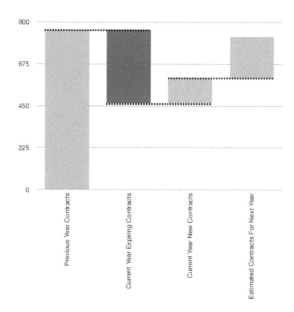

Labels are hard to read and too long. Keeping the category labels short will help illustrate the presenter's message.

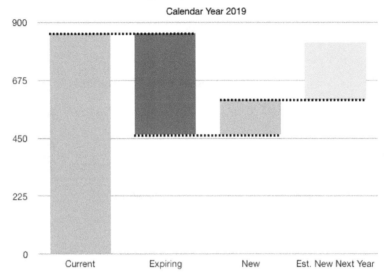

Legal Department Contracts
Calendar Year 2019

Labels are simplified with the addition of a title explaining the subject. Any estimated should be a lighter color.

• **Consistent Color:** Keeping the positive and negative movements on the graph, a consistent color helps the audience. Too much variation in color will muddle the presenter's message.

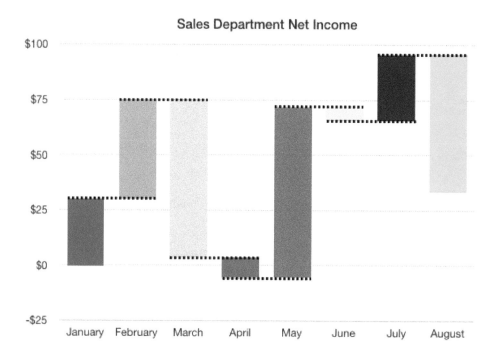

Inconsistent color creates a busy graph.

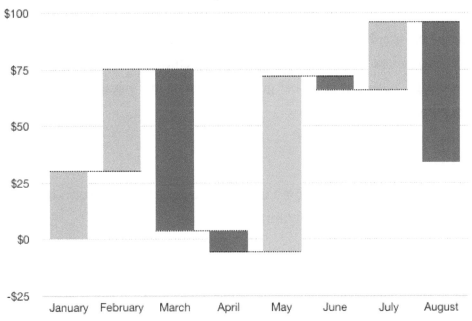

Clearer graph with consistent color and smaller leader lines.

Stacked Bar/Column Graph

Stacked bar graphs are great to show multiple data points in one single category. Stacked bar graphs can quickly become cluttered and lose their intended message. Keep the stack bar graphs simple by limiting the number of data points.

Styling

- **Categories:** Graphs with more than 5-7 categories become convoluted. Keep the graph simple with limited categories.

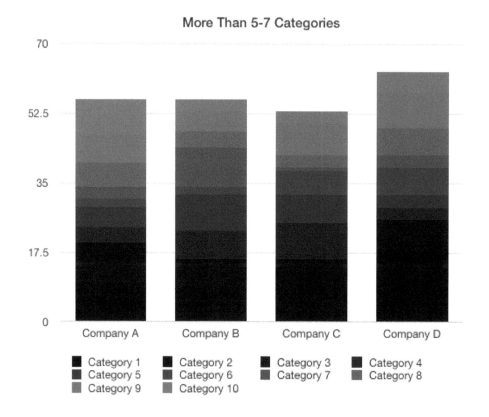

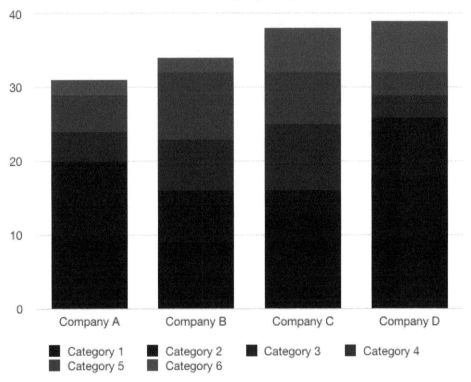

6 Category Graph

- **Zebra-ing:** Zebra-ing, or color stripping, is upsetting to the eye. Keep the colors within the same palette.

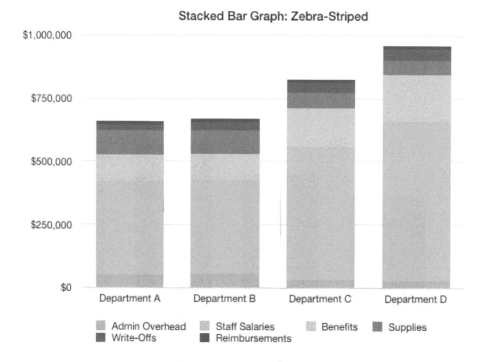

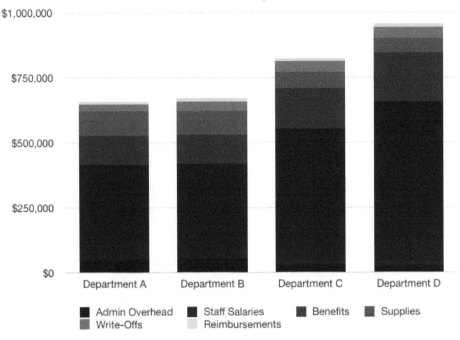

Stacked Bar Graph: Same Pallet

- **Ordering:** Order the graphs from the largest category at the bottom and smallest at the top.

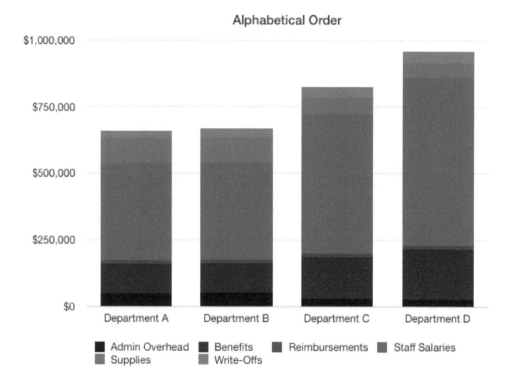

Descending Order

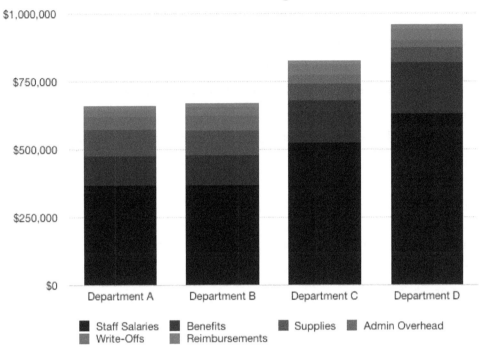

Area Graph

Area graphs are great at showing combined trends over time. This graph shows part-to-whole relationships by showing volume as well as change over time. Because the area graph is communicating trends over time vs. individual data points, using this graph correctly can make a compelling overall story. There are three types of area charts: standard, stacked, and 100% stacked.

Standard

Standard Area Graphs are best used to show or compare progression over time. If many data points are to be graphed, it may be better to display on a lined graph instead.

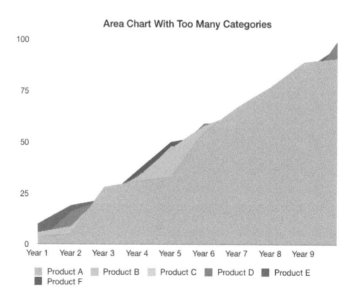

With this many categories, a line graph would better represent the presenter's message.

- **Transparency:** When using a standard area graph, set the transparency on the first graphs, and set the farthest back graph to a black/grey color. It is helpful to have the front visuals primary colors, so when they overlap, they create another color. Having the farthest back color a dark grey or black helps by not interfere with the mixing of the transparent colors.

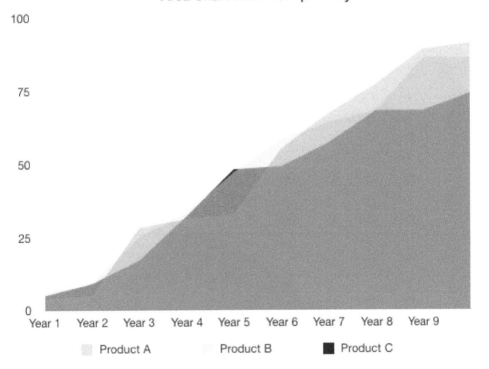

When the blue and yellow overlap, they create a green graph that can be differentiated between the other colors.

Stacked

Stacked area graphs are best used to visualize part-to-whole relationships with each of the categories. By adding each category on top of the others help show how each category contributes to the cumulative total.

For both stacked and 100% stacked area graphs, use a color pallet that will show differentiation for each of the categories. Colors too similar will hinder the message and confuse the audience.

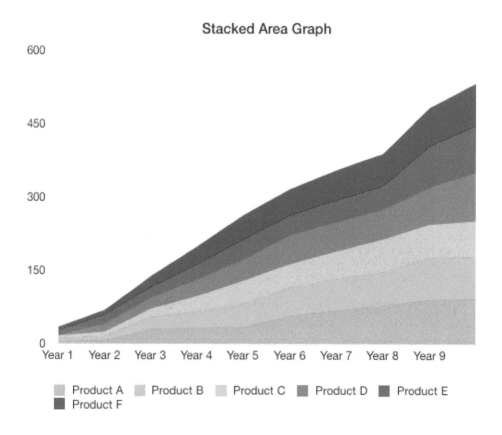

Stacked Area Graph

100% Stacked

100% stacked area graphs are best used to show the distribution of categories as parts of a whole, where the cumulative total is unimportant. Showing trends over time as a percentage of the total.

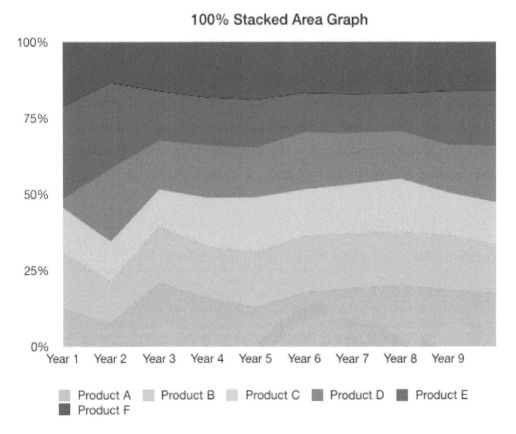

100% Stacked Area Graph

Pie/Doughnut Charts

There is a debate among data professionals about the use of pie and dough-nut charts. On one side of the argument is these types of graphs should never be utilized because they are overused, and the data could be visually displayed in a more meaningful format. Others are of the opinion that pie charts are fine to use sparingly for quick information.

Most of the time, pie charts could be put into a simple text or stacked bar chart. Pie charts are very narrow in focus. They can only show percentages of a snapshot of data, where a stacked bar chart can show percentages over time. Doughnut charts can be substituted but in limited circumstances, and if the decision is between and pie and a doughnut chart, choose pie.

Basics Styling

• **Ordering/Sorting:** Order clockwise from greatest to least.

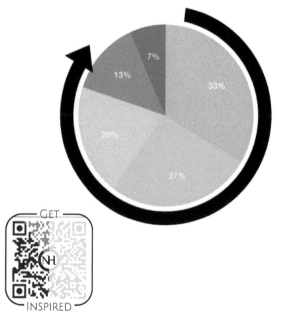

- **Coloring:** The audience should be able to distinguish between colors. Colors that are too close together or colors that "clash" are hard to read. Highlight important parts of the pie.

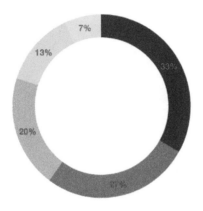

A green background with red text is hard to read.

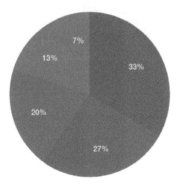

There is not enough change in the section color to identify where the pie pieces separate.

• **Slicing:** When there is a need to show more information from a slice of the original whole, most people will show a pie within a pie, which is challenging to grasp and too much work for the audience to compare to the first pie. Make it more interesting by adding a bar chart to show more information.

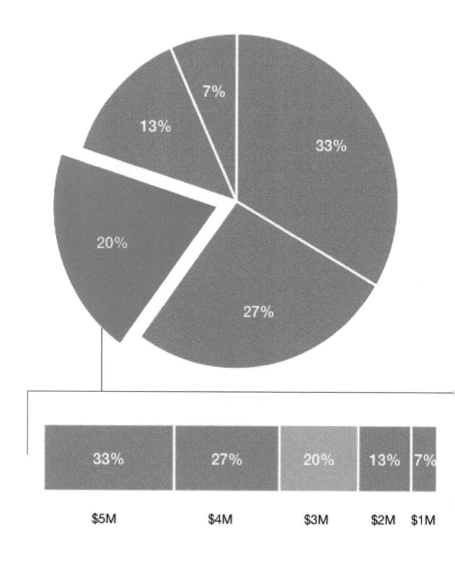

- **Sizing:** When showing proportional sizes, use the total area instead of the radius. This requires a little bit of math (Area $= \pi r^2$).

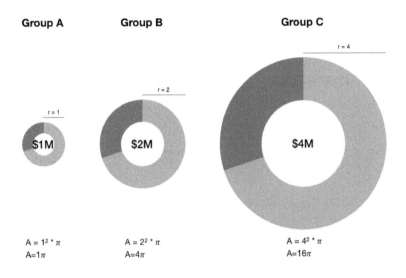

Incorrect proportions increase the area size exponentially.

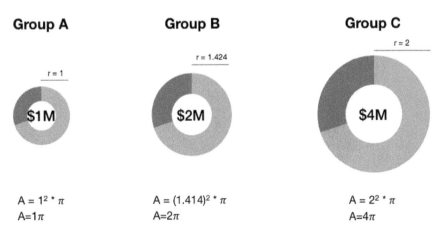

Correct proportions of the pie area.

Pie Chart Alternatives

Most times, instead of using a pie chart, another chart would have a more meaningful impact. This section will look at a few examples that could be used instead.

- **Simple Text/Pictograph:** The most common use for the pie chart is showing gender. Showing the discrepancy of gender in a simple text or pictograph is more interesting to the audience. It can grab the viewer's attention better than a pie chart they have seen many times.

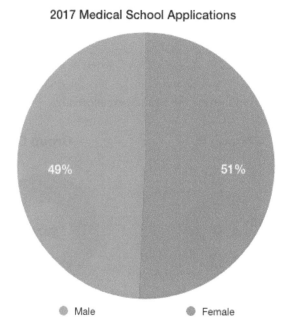

2017 Medical School Applications

49%   51%

● Male   ● Female

-

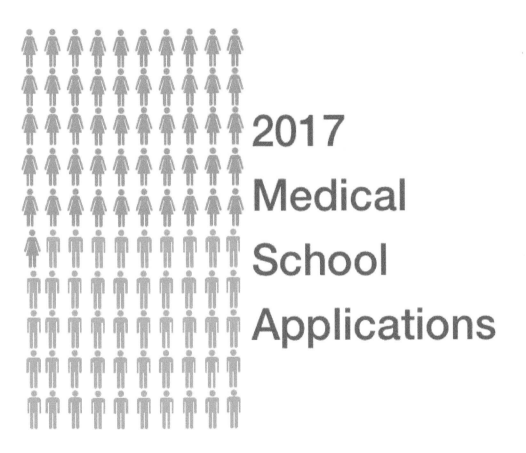

2017 Medical School Applications

Both of these graphs show the same information. Which one grabs your attention?

- **Trending:** Showing trending data is better presented in a stacked bar chart rather than a pie chart.

Historical Medical School Applications by Gender

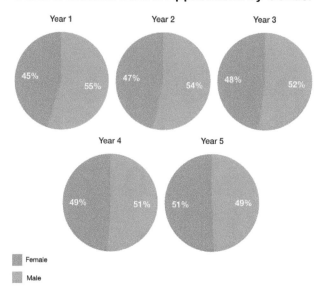

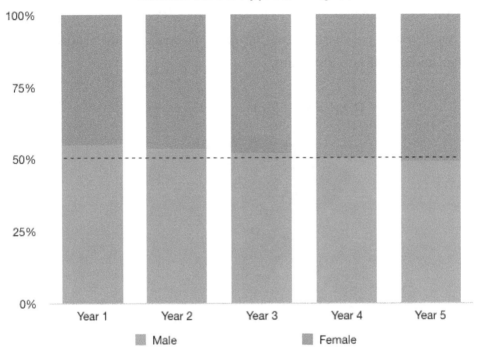

Medical School Application by Gender

Legend: Male | Female

- **KPIs:** When showing a KPI that reflects a level that is needed to be successful, e.x. production needs to have less than 10% defects, a gage would be better than a pie chart. Gages are easier to understand the goal, current value, and out-of-bounds values.

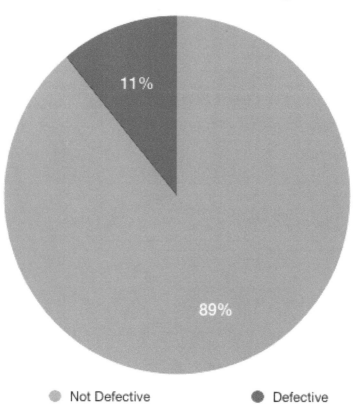

Production Defective Percentage

11%

89%

Not Defective   Defective

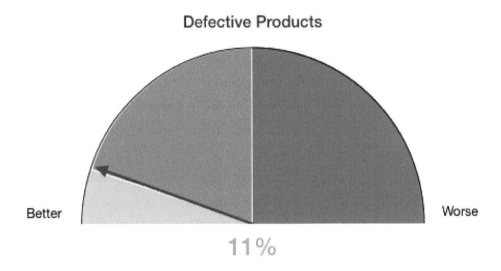

Defective Products

Better

Worse

11%

Clusters

With the explosion of data science, AI, and neural networks, clustering graphs are being integrated more in every aspect of business decision making. Cluster graphs are a way for data scientists to understand what is going on with the data and design their models more effectively. These scientists keep evaluating and changing their data model to better identify trends and classifications. As businesses become more competitive, these types of graphs, and the implications behind them, are becoming indispensable. Cluster graphs are dependent of identified nodes. Nodes are the center of the clusters. There can be many nodes or 1 node, depending on how the data model was created. A node of 1 can be possible but won't necessarily show sophisticated insights. Graphs that have a high count of nodes will not necessarily give better ideas. The following example will be looking at a nearest neighbor data model (or k-nearest neighbor, KNN). These skills can be applied to other types of cluster graphs.

100 Node Cluster Graph

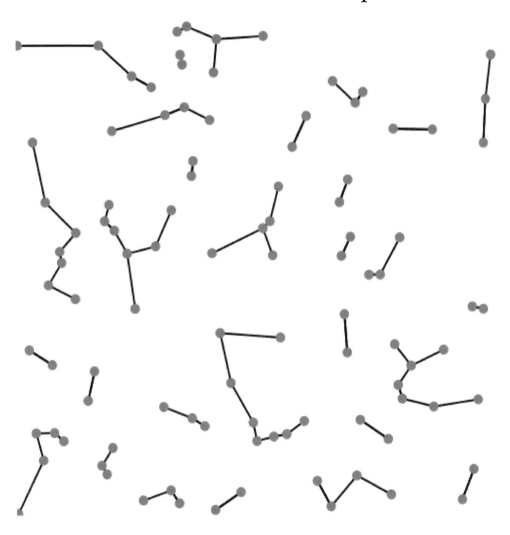

Styling

- **Define Clusters:** Using the proximity, closure, and common region as a guide, define clusters visually. The graph below is the raw data of a clustering project. Just by looking at it, there is no meaning.

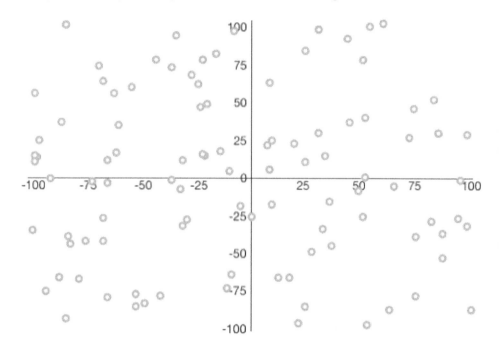

Basic cluster graph with no common region, proximity, or closure principals applied.

By using the common region principle to identify areas of meaning, the audience can understand the message of this graph without the presenter going into exact details and possibly losing the focus of the audience.

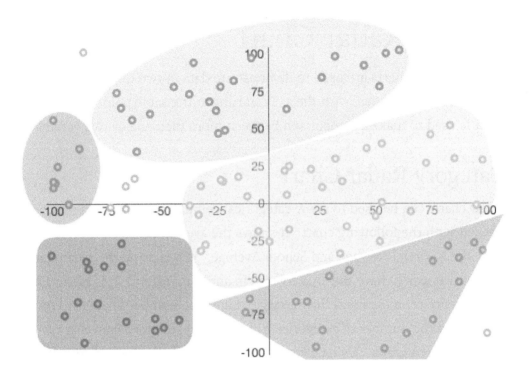

Clustering graph with common regional principal applied.

When the principal of common region is applied, the graphs show 5 different areas of meaning as well as some outliers. The presenter can go into more detail for each of the areas (some more significant than others).

Spider/Radar Chart

Radar (Spider) charts are used to demonstrate data in two dimensions for two or more data series, with the axes starting at the same point. A radar chart is used to make a comparison between more than one or two variables.

Category Radar Chart

Radar charts can be used to show categorical comparisons. Parents may be familiar with the following chart. It shows the average score for each category by the National Average and School Average. When using the radar chart to show categories have the area colored in and transparent. It is easier for the audience to understand the message. Limit the number of areas to two to four and the number of categories from three to 15, more than that creates a cluttered graph. Using a complementary or triadic color scheme helps the information stand on its own.

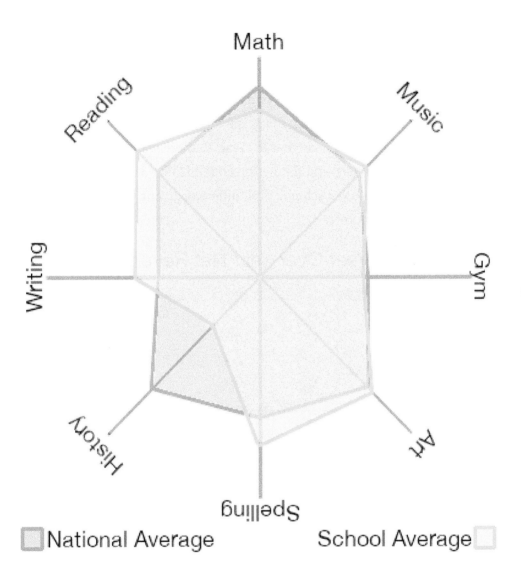

Math

Music

Reading

Gym

Writing

History

Art

Spelling

National Average   School Average

Continuous Radar Graph

The other use for a radar graph is by a continuous category or any category that can be summarized by time (seconds, minutes, hours, days, months, years, process order, etc.). Below, the graph shows net revenue by month for each year. The audience can see that in 'Year 2', there was a big jump in net revenue starting in January and flat net revenue in 'Year 3'. With the lines being close together, a color scheme with different greens helps the audience differentiate the data points.

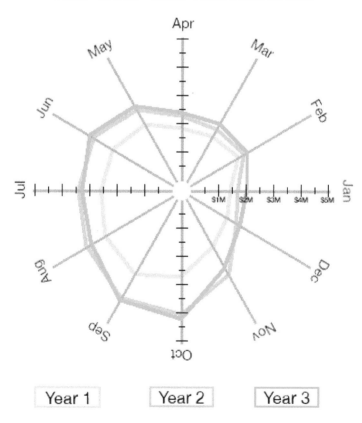

Year Over Year Net Revenue

Maps & GIS

Businesses can utilize public information to leverage business strategies using a GIS or a map to show areas of opportunity. GIS can show a broad national view and can be drilled down to zip, or even census tract, level. These types of graphics are becoming more predominant in strategic business planning because of the level of detail they provide. With such detail increases the chances of clutter and distraction.

What is GIS?

GIS, or geographic information system, is a way of displaying data on top of a map to organize, analyze, and communicate the science of the world. Rooted in the science of geography, GIS integrates many types of data. It analyzes the spatial location and organizes layers of information into visualizations using maps and 3D scenes. With this unique capability, GIS reveals more in-depth insights into data, such as patterns, relationships, and situations—helping users make smarter decisions.

With GIS, businesses can identify problems, monitor changes, manage and respond to natural disasters, forecasting, define priorities, and understand trends. Prominent data sets are available free from federal, state, and local governments. Sources include everything from national census data to New

York taxi trips. www.Data.Gov is an excellent resource with over 250,000+ datasets.

History of GIS

GIS started in the 1960s as computers and early concepts of quantitative and computational geography emerged. The academic community was early adopters of GIS for research. Later, the National Center for Geographic Information and Analysis formalized research on key geographic information science topics such as spatial analysis and visualization. These efforts fueled a quantitative revolution in the world of geographic science and laid the groundwork for GIS.

The Canada Geographic Information System created in the first computerized GIS in the world in 1963. The Canadian government had commissioned them to create a manageable inventory of its natural resources, envisioning using computers to merge natural resource data from all provinces. The design for automated computing to store and process large amounts of data, which enabled Canada to begin its national land-use management program, we developed and named GIS.

By the end of the 20th century, the rapid growth in various systems had been consolidated and standardized on relatively few platforms, and users were beginning to explore viewing GIS data over the Internet, requiring data format and transfer standards. More recently, a growing number of free, open-source GIS packages run on a range of operating systems and can be customized to perform specific tasks.

GIS Styling

GIS maps can show a lot of information in a single snapshot. This type of graph can become cluttered and overwhelming to the audience.

- **Keep Background Simple:** Unless there is a need for roads, railways, waterways, or any geographic markings, keep them off the map. Maps should just have a simple background that shows boundaries for cities, states, metropolitan statistical areas (MSA), or business areas. If you have the option, a darker background is easier to read than a light background.

Interstates, roads, train tracks, national parks, and waterways create a busy background.

A simple background with contrasting label color is easier to read.

- **Zoom:** Zoom into the area that shows the data. Too macro of a view is difficult to understand, and too micro of a view cuts off essential data. A city map should be zoomed to the boundaries of the city, not the nation, and a nation map should be zoomed to the edges of the nation, and not the world.

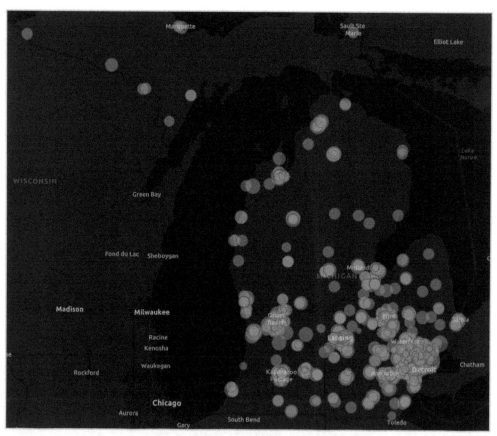

Specific address data from Michigan shows clustering around city centers. The message is that cities are more populated, which is common knowledge.

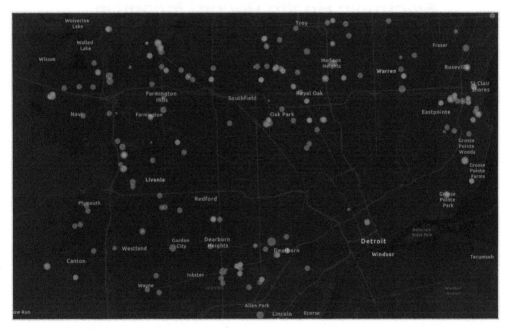

Correct zoom tells a story that most points of contact are in the suburbs and not downtown, pre-venting a disastrous business decision to move into downtown.

Filled Map

Filled maps shows a great deal of information in one single snapshot. Coloring is important with filled maps as to not get too confusing. Using a gradation key is helpful. For more detailed information, adding a data table is useful.

Center for Medicare and Medicaid Services Electronic Health Record Incentive Reimbursement Payments 2014

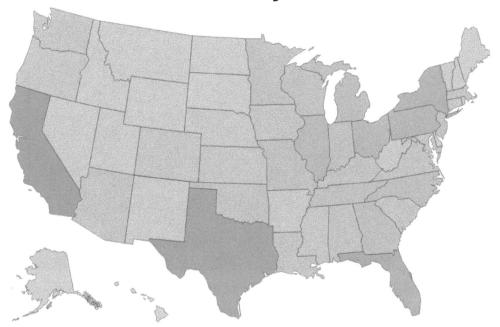

Without any details, this map has no message.

Center for Medicare and Medicaid Services
Electronic Health Record Incentive
Reimbursement Payments 2014

State	Payments	State	Payments
Alabama	$174M	Montana	$43M
Alaska	$13M	Nebraska	$86M
Arizona	$155M	Nevada	$44M
Arkansas	$98M	New Hampshire	$34M
California	$642M	New Jersey	$211M
Colorado	$110M	New Mexico	$60M
Connecticut	$82M	New York	$439M
Delaware	$22M	North Carolina	$272M
District Of Columbia	$19M	North Dakota	$64M
Florida	$487M	Ohio	$356M
Georgia	$242M	Oklahoma	$165M
Hawaii	$21M	Oregon	$106M
Idaho	$32M	Pennsylvania	$399M
Illinois	$350M	Puerto Rico	$3M
Indiana	$192M	Rhode Island	$14M
Iowa	$134M	South Carolina	$146M
Kansas	$119M	South Dakota	$39M
Kentucky	$143M	Tennessee	$227M
Louisiana	$166M	Texas	$599M
Maine	$36M	Utah	$66M
Maryland	$153M	Vermont	$20M
Massachusetts	$175M	Virginia	$188M
Michigan	$297M	Washington	$152M
Minnesota	$185M	West Virginia	$77M
Mississippi	$117M	Wisconsin	$202M
Missouri	$234M	Wyoming	$24M

$3 M $642 M

Adding a gradation key and data table creates a helpful map.

- **Layering:** GIS use data as layers, and each layer stacks on top of the previous layers. Keep layers simple. Too many layers, or datasets, are cluttering and confusing.

  Also, limit the type of data categories. A single data element, for example, Household Income, can be a gradient layer where a categorical data type, male/female, can be a pie chart. A dataset that has multiple categories, like the census defined race, is better in separate filled maps.

Bubble Map

Bubble maps are great at showing total sum within a specific area. Bubbles may overlap and cover up other bubbles. Setting transparency to the bubbles makes it easier to see all data points.

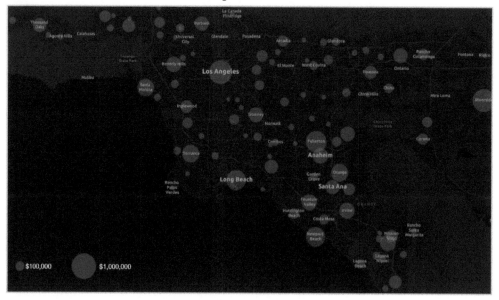

Adding a bubble key helps with understanding the total sum for the bubble area.

Pie Map

Similar to the bubble map, the size of the pie chart shows the sum of the specific area. Too many categories displayed within the chart on the map is harmful to the overall message. Keep things simple by limiting to three to five categories.

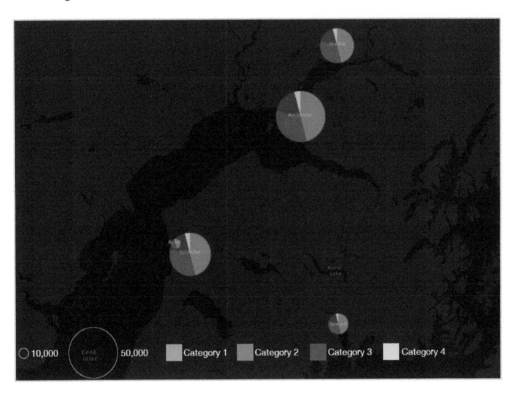

Pictograph

Pictographs can transform data into an engaging story. Pictographs are icons, images, or symbols and are used to depict quantitative information. Not all data can be transformed into pictographs. Pictographs work best as quick snapshots of quantity and volume. A compelling visual is engaging, and the audience can quickly compare the snapshot.

Icons

Icons in pictographs should be simple and remain clear and crisp when reduced to small size. Icons with too much detail do not scale well and can hinder the reader from comparing the underlying data. Symbols that are roughly in a square shape work better in a pictograph.

Variations

When the perfect icon is selected, that icon should represent all data within that pictograph. Combining different icons is very distracting and hard for the viewer to compare the underlying data. The pictograph should focus the reader on the information and not the icons.

Simple Icons	Too Detailed

Quantity

Do the math for the audience, don't have them count every single icon to interpret the visual. Avoid partial symbols and uncommon units. A bar graph may be a better option to display. Natural denominations include 1,2,5,10,50 and 100.

Account Types

Different icons create distractions

Account Types

One icon with different shading

Complicated Partial Symbols

 = 5

 9

 18

24

Unnatural Denominations

 = 3

 9

 18

24

Natural Denominations

 = 10

 30

 60

 80

CHAPTER 5

How-to Charts

Let's get into some charts! The following pages will help you get on your way to making top-notch, presentation-quality charts. Each section shows steps on how to replicate the chart. Below is an example of a terrible chart, displaying some basics steps that should be followed when making any charts for presentations.

Background

This ugly graph has a hideous background color. The color only distracts from what the presenter is trying to convey. Remove all color and make the background transparent. If the space you are working with does not react well to a transparent background, then change the background color too white or a light gray. In this example, the background color of red will be changed to transparent.

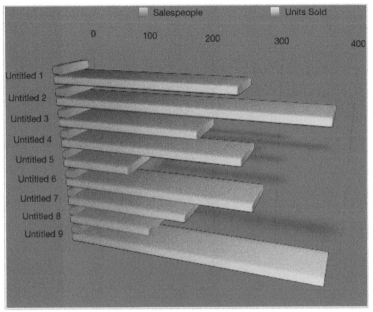

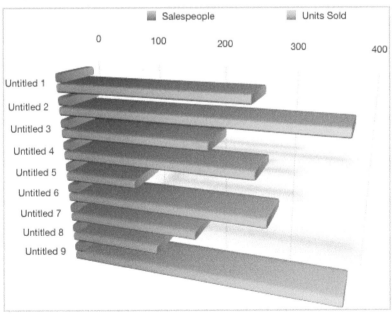

3D

No, just don't. 3D should not be used for graphs, it's too confusing and distracting. 3D graphs have gone by way of 3D TVs and Red/Blue paper glasses. 2D graphs are better at communicating your ideas.

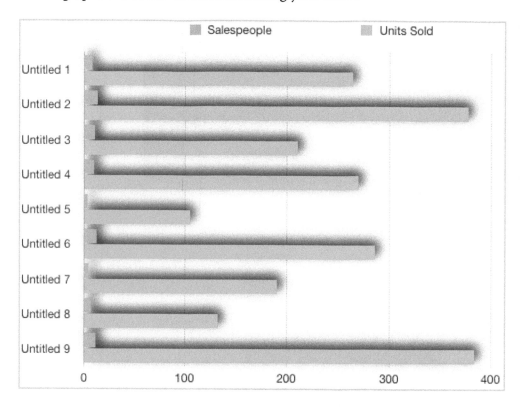

Styling

Remove all styling. Borders, shadows, outlines, major and minor grid lines. Removing all of these items makes a cleaner graph, and it helps your audience focus on the data instead of deciphering the information.

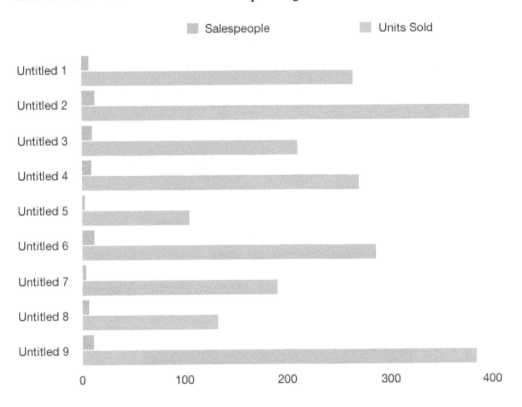

Labels, Legends, and Titles

This graph has come quite a ways from its hideous start, but it still does not tell a clear story or idea. Add labels as needed to make sure the audience understands what you are trying to convey. Remove legends if they are redundant. More than one data source can keep the legend. Create a title that shows what the audience needs to understand. In this example, the salespeople category did not add value as a bar and was added to the labels. This information is still relevant in later steps and will be kept with the graph.

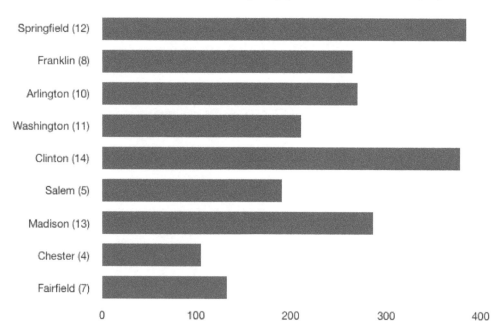

141

Sorting

Sorting the chart makes a big difference with how your audience understands your message. You spend just a fraction of a second too long figuring
out which ones are outliers. Instead, you should reorder your data points to
go from largest to smallest. Most of the modern languages of Europe, North
and South America, India, and Southeast Asia are written left to right and
top to bottom. Your graphs should follow the same format. Larger data at
the top (or left) and smaller at the bottom (or right).

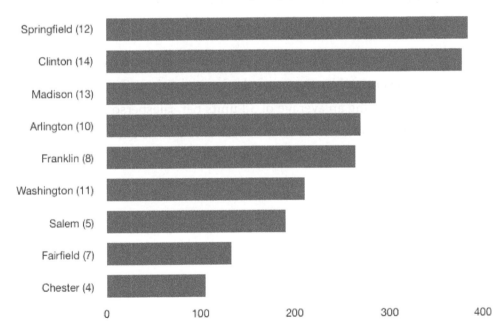

Total Units Sold by City (Number Of Sales People)

The Point

This chart has gone through a considerable transformation for the better. You could present the graph as is, but what is the point? Springfield sold more units? Chester sold the least? Your audience could get the same information from a table, and you wouldn't have to go through all the work to make a graph. The opportunity to tell a story and become a presentation champ is what you do next. There is hidden information within the data that is not being highlighted. Springfield sold more units, but they had 12 salespeople. Springfield was more efficient than Clinton with 14 salespeople. Which city was able to sell the most units with the fewest number of sales staff and thus was the most useful.

Changing the colors and highlighting your idea benefits the story overall. You can now present and let the graph do the explaining. Salem was the most efficient by selling an average of 38 units per salesperson. The color change adds another dimension to the chart. It is drastic enough to focus the audience's gaze on that data point of the graph.

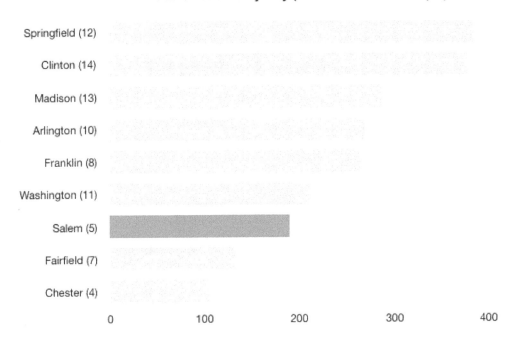

Total Units Sold by City (Number Of Sales People)

The following graphs have instructions on how to create that exact look. These should be used as a starting point for your graphs. Expand on these ideas and make them your own.

Line Chart

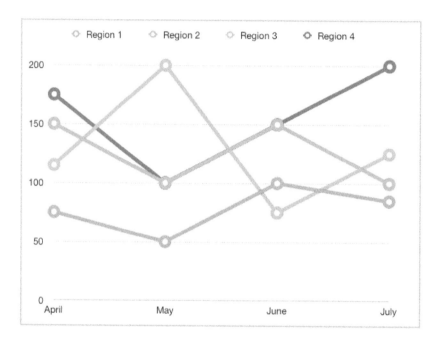

The problem with this graph is all the data is shown without a narrative. If the purpose is to show all the data use a table instead. This graph is cluttered, distracting from any point the presenter is trying to get the audience to understand. Below is a graph that helps the presenter narrate their idea, and it also helps the audience know why they are being shown this presentation.

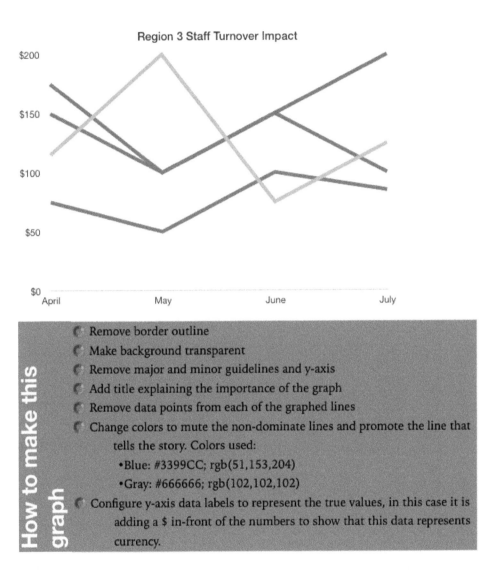

Region 3 Staff Turnover Impact

How to make this graph

- Remove border outline
- Make background transparent
- Remove major and minor guidelines and y-axis
- Add title explaining the importance of the graph
- Remove data points from each of the graphed lines
- Change colors to mute the non-dominate lines and promote the line that tells the story. Colors used:
  - Blue: #3399CC; rgb(51,153,204)
  - Gray: #666666; rgb(102,102,102)
- Configure y-axis data labels to represent the true values, in this case it is adding a $ in-front of the numbers to show that this data represents currency.

As you can see, the graph is cleaner and easier to understand than the original graph. There was turnover in Region 3, which leads to a steep decline in June, and the problem has been remedied in July. Your audience will appreciate the straightforward nature of this type of presentation where they can garner understanding and be able to provide poignant feedback.

Scatter Plot

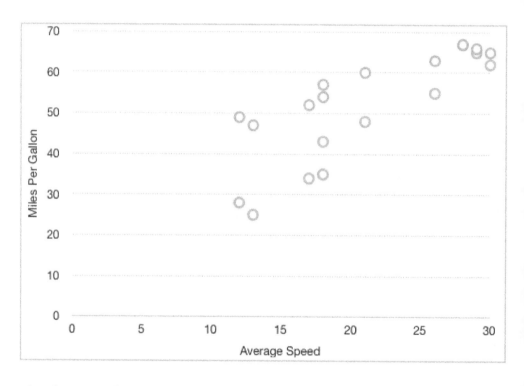

The above graph gives enough information, but it can be better. Making the relevant category a bold color highlights the message. Using a crosshair instead of a circle gives a more accurate picture of the data point.

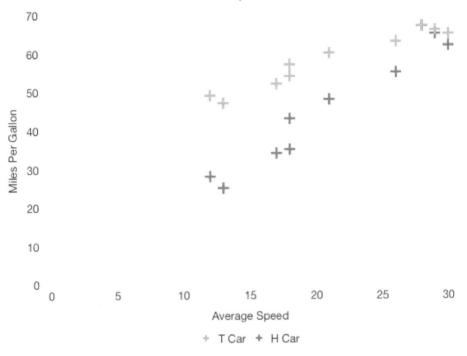

H Car Compared to T Car

How to make this graph

- Remove border outline
- Make background transparent
- Remove major and minor guidelines and y-axis
- Add title and key
- More finite data points
- Change colors to mute the non-dominate data points and promote the data points that tells the story. Colors used:
    - Orange: #E88A47; rgb(255,158,65)
    - Gray: #89847F; rgb(137,132,127)

Bubble Chart

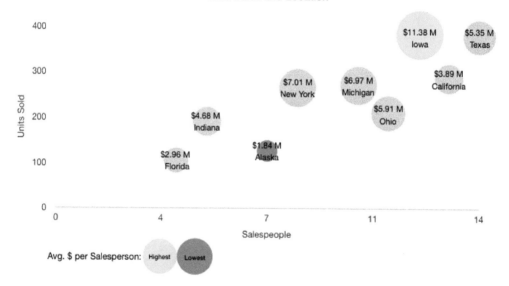

Total Sales and Location

Units Sold

- $11.38 M Iowa
- $5.35 M Texas
- $7.01 M New York
- $6.97 M Michigan
- $3.89 M California
- $5.91 M Ohio
- $4.68 M Indiana
- $1.84 M Alaska
- $2.96 M Florida

Salespeople

0   4   7   11   14

Avg. $ per Salesperson: Highest Lowest

- Remove border outline
- Make background transparent
- Remove major and minor guidelines and y-axis
- Add title and key
- Define the important parts by highlighting in contrasting colors
- Colors used:
    - Purple: #531B93; rgb(83,27,147); 60% opacity
    - Red: #E32400; rgb(227,36,0); 60% opacity
    - Green: #00F900; rgb(0,249,0); 60% opacity

Horizontal Bar Graph

Units Sold by Sales Person

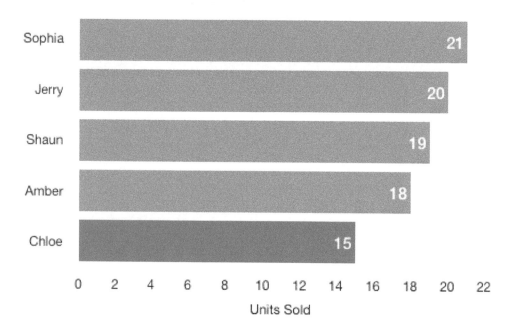

- Remove border outline
- Make background transparent
- Remove major and minor guidelines and y-axis
- Order by descending total units sold
- Define the important parts by highlighting in contrasting colors
- Colors used:
  - Gray: #A9A9A9; rgb(169,169,169);
  - Salmon: #FC5937; rgb(252,89,55); 90% opacity

Vertical Bar Graph

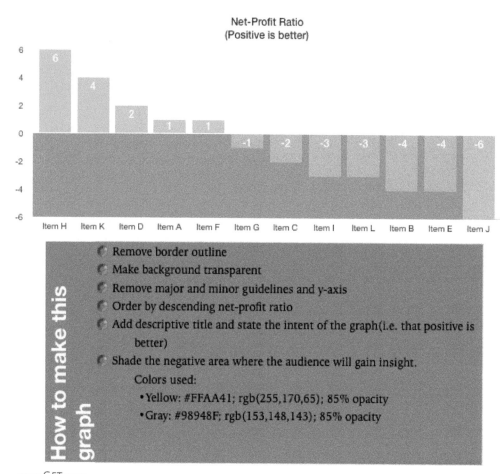

Net-Profit Ratio
(Positive is better)

How to make this graph

- Remove border outline
- Make background transparent
- Remove major and minor guidelines and y-axis
- Order by descending net-profit ratio
- Add descriptive title and state the intent of the graph(i.e. that positive is better)
- Shade the negative area where the audience will gain insight.
  - Colors used:
    - Yellow: #FFAA41; rgb(255,170,65); 85% opacity
    - Gray: #98948F; rgb(153,148,143); 85% opacity

Waterfall Chart

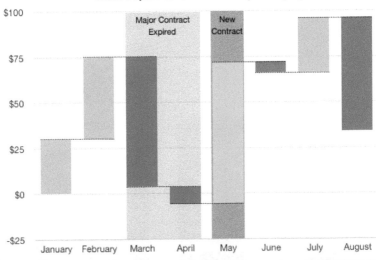

Sales Department Net Income per Employee

How to make this graph

- Remove border outline
- Make background transparent
- Remove minor guidelines and y-axis, keeping major guidelines
- Add leader lines between categories that are different in color and thickness than any major guidelines
- Add descriptive title and text with shading explaining any abnormalities in the data
- Keep positive all the same color and all the negative the same color
    Colors used:
    - Green: #6EBB46; rgb(110,187,70);
    - Red: #FF2600; rgb(255,38,0);
    - Light Gray Box: #D6D6D6; rgb(214,214,214);
    - Dark Gray Box: #A9A9A9; rgb(169,169,169);

SECTION 7

Stacked Column

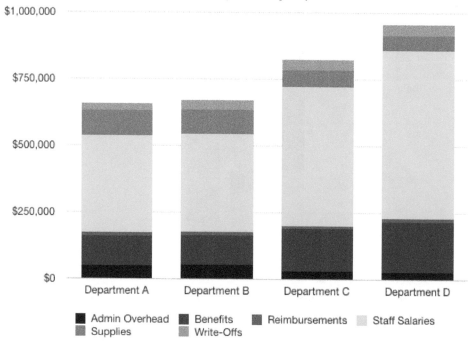

2019 Expenses by Department

- Remove border outline
- Make background transparent
- Remove minor guidelines and y-axis, keeping major guidelines
- Order categories alphabetically
- Highlight area of importance
- Add descriptive title

Colors used:

- Staff Salaries: #00F900; rgb(0,249,0);
- Admin Overhead: #424242; rgb(66,66,66);
- Benefits: #5E5E5E; rgb(94,94,94);
- Reimbursements: #797979; rgb(121,121,121);
- Supplies: #919191; rgb(145,145,145);
- Write-Offs: #A9A9A9; rgb(169,169,169);

Stacked Row

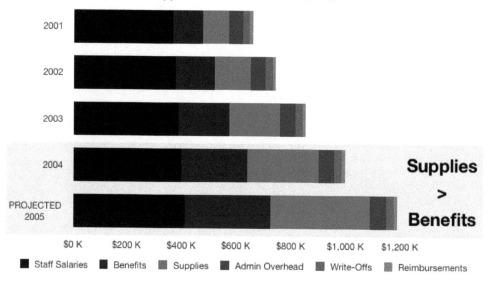

Department A Expenses
Supplies Growth 30% Year Over Year

- 2001
- 2002
- 2003
- 2004
- PROJECTED 2005

$0 K $200 K $400 K $600 K $800 K $1,000 K $1,200 K

■ Staff Salaries   ■ Benefits   ■ Supplies   ■ Admin Overhead   ■ Write-Offs   ■ Reimbursements

Supplies
>
Benefits

- Remove border outline
- Make background transparent
- Remove all guidelines and y-axis
- Order categories by value
- Highlight area that tells the story
- Add descriptive title that defines the story
  Colors used:
    - Supplies: #9437FF; rgb(148,55,255);
    - Staff Salaries: #212121; rgb(33,33,33);
    - Benefits: #424242; rgb(66,66,66);
    - Admin Overhead: #5E5E5E; rgb(94,94,94);
    - Write-Offs: #797979; rgb(121,121,121);
    - Reimbursements: #929292; rgb(146,146,146);

Pie Charts

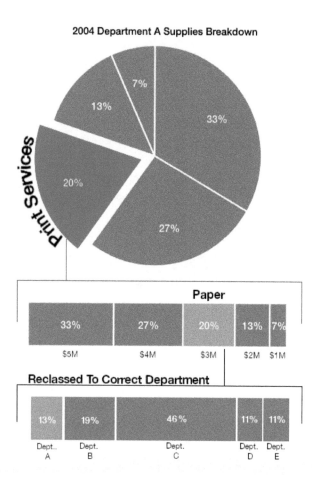

2004 Department A Supplies Breakdown

- Remove border outline
- Add spacers between each category and breakout the important slice
- Add a bar showing more details and highlight important piece
- This graph shows that Department A had paper supplies from other departments assigned to them and then reclassified to the correct department.
- Add descriptive titles at every step of the process

  Colors used:
  - Print Services: #1B49FB; rgb(27,73.251);
  - Paper: #F09133; rgb(240,145,51);
  - Other: #909190; rgb(144,145,144);

GET
NH
INSPIRED

Cluster Graph

Customer Spend, Time Clustered by Store
Difference From Store Average

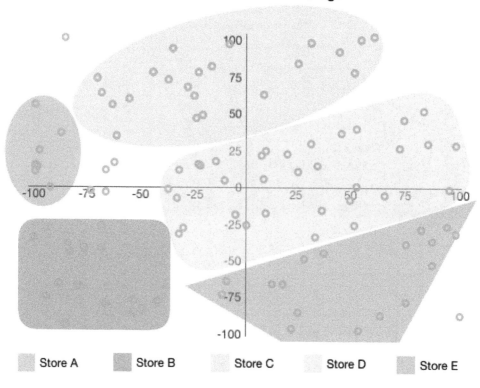

Store A   Store B   Store C   Store D   Store E

- Remove border outline.
- Add transparent background.
- Identify the clusters with different colors.
- Understand the outliers and be able to speak to them
- Add key at the bottom of the graph.
- Add a descriptive title

  Colors used:
  - Store A: #005493; rgb(0,84,147); 32% opacity
  - Store B: #941751; rgb(148,23,81); 32% opacity
  - Store C: #FF9300; rgb(255,147,0); 25% opacity
  - Store D: #00F900; rgb(0,249,0); 35% opacity
  - Store E: #919191; rgb(145,145,145); 45% opacity
  - Data Point: #2E578C; rgb(46,87,140);

CHAPTER 6

Don't Stop!

The Data Spectrum

Data started with paper, a pencil, and a ruler. Then computers came and introduced spreadsheets and transformed how corporations did business. Data is still changing. Now instead of spreadsheets, there are big data warehouses, data marts, and data lakes. These vast databases hold massive amounts of data that need to be analyzed and displayed to understand underlying trends hidden within the data. Artificial intelligence loves all this data. Machines learning has taken off in the past few years where because of all the data that is available.

As business progress into the data spectrum, the need for data individuals has increased. These data-minded people can make sense of all the information and present it coherently. Executives need results that they can understand and be able to take action. Gone are the days of printed spreadsheets and mediocre charts. Data is transforming, and it is an exciting time to be involved in its evolution. Keep learning and expanding on your data knowledge. Data presenting from 5 years ago is vastly different than today. Imagine what it will be in the next 5 years.

More Resources

There are more resources at NickHobbie.com. Examples of graphs and other tools to help you be successful. Keep checking back for updates on new graph templates and color schemes. When you are ready, use #RateMyGraph on social to get feedback on your work.

Twitter: @NickHobbie

IG: @Nick.Hobbie

BIBLIOGRAPHY

Albers, Josef. Interaction of Color. Yale University Press, 2006.

Bellantoni, Patti. If Its Purple, Someones Gonna Die: the Power of Color in Visual Storytelling for Film. Focal Press, 2005.

Berry, Joseph K. Beyond Mapping: Concepts, Algorithms, and Issues in GIS. GIS World, Inc., 1993.

Bolstad, Paul. GIS Fundamentals: a First Text on Geographic Information Systems. Eider Press, 2005.

Burchett, K. E. "Color harmony". Color Research and Application, 27 (1), 2002, pp. 28–31.

Buzai, Gustavo D., and David J. Robinson. "Geographical Information Systems (GIS) in Latin America, 1987-2010: A Preliminary Overview." Journal of Latin American Geography, vol. 9, no. 3, 2010, pp. 9–31., doi:10.1353/lag.2010.0027.

Chibana, Nayomi. "Color Theory for Presentations: How to Choose the Perfect Colors for Your Designs." Visual Learning Center by Visme, https://visme.co/blog/how-to-choose-a-color-scheme/#SOJqsBdAdL34sFX4.99.

Chang, Kang-Tsung. Introduction to Geographic Information Systems. McGraw-Hill, 2010.

Elangovan, K. GIS: Fundamentals, Applications and Implementations. New India Publ. Agency, 2006.

Feisner, E. A. Colour: How to use colour in art and design. London: Laurence King, 2000.

Fu, Pinde, and Jiulin Sun. Web GIS: Principles and Applications. ESRI Press, 2011.

Garau, Augusto. Color Harmonies. University of Chicago Press, 1993.

Hard, A. & Sivik, L. "A theory of colors in combination – A descriptive model related to the NCS color-order system". Color Research and Application, 26 (1), 2001, pp. 4–28.

Harvey, Francis. "A Primer of GIS: Fundamental Geographic and Cartographic Concepts." The Guilford Press, vol. 46, no. 01, Jan. 2008, p. 31.

Heywood, Ian, et al. An Introduction to Geographical Information Systems. Pearson, 2011.

"History of GIS: Early History and the Future of GIS." Esri, https://www.esri.com/en-us/what-is-gis/history-of-gis.

John, De Smith Michael, et al. Geospatial Analysis: a Comprehensive Guide to Principles, Techniques and Software Tools. Matador, 2009.

Longley, Paul, et al. Geographic Information Systems Science. 2nd ed., Chichester: Wiley, 2005.

King-Theme.com. "Your Guide to Colors: Color Theory, The Color Wheel, & How to Choose a Color Scheme." Network Marketing, 4 Oct. 2018, https://godspeednetwork.com/your-guide-to-colors-color-theory-the-color-wheel-how-to-choose-a-color-scheme/.

Knaflic, Cole Nussbaumer. Storytelling with Data: a Data Visualization Guide for Business Professionals. Wiley, 2015.

Lundquist, Samual. "33 Beautiful Color Combinations for Your next Design." 99designs, 99designs, 6 Sept. 2019, https://99designs.com/blog/creative-inspiration/color-combinations/.

Mahnke, F. Color, environment and human response. New York: John Wiley & Sons, 1996.

Maliene, Vida, et al. "Geographic Information System: Old Principles with New Capabilities." URBAN DESIGN International, vol. 16, no. 1, 2011, pp. 1–6., doi:10.1057/udi.2010.25.

Mcdonnell, Rachael. Principles of Geographical Information Systems. Oxford University Press, 1998.

Mennecke, Brian E., and Lawrence A. West Jr. "Geographic Information Systems in Developing Countries." Journal of Global Information Management, vol. 9, no. 4, 2001, pp. 44–54., doi:10.4018/jgim.2001100103.

O'Connor, Z. "Color harmony revisited". Color Research and Application, 35 (4), 2010, pp. 267–273.

O'Connor, Z. "Colour psychology and colour therapy: Caveat emptor". Color Research and Application, 2010.

Ott, Thomas, and Frank Swiaczny. "Processing and Analysis of Spatio-Temporal Data inside a GIS." Time-Integrative Geographic Information Systems, 2001, pp. 127–141., doi:10.1007/978-3-642-56747-6_5.

Packaging, Fox. "Color Theory Part 1: Introduction to Color Theory in Packaging." Fox News, https://blog.foxbag.com/color-theory-part-1-introduction-to-color-theory-in-packaging.

Pointer, M. R. & Attridge, G.G. "The number of discernible colors". Color Research and Application, 23 (1), 1998, pp. 52–54.

Rsgisworld. "History of GIS; Beginning to Now Journey of Geographical Information System." Remote Sensing and GIS World, Blogger, 10 Jan. 2019, https://www.rsgisworld.com/2019/01/history-of-gis-beginning-to-now-journey.html.

Wong, Dona M. The Wall Street Journal Guide to Information Graphics: the Dos and Donts of Presenting Data, Facts, and Figures. Norton, 2013.

Zelazny, Gene. *Say It with Charts: the Executives Guide to Visual Communication.* McGraw-Hill, 1996.